William
STYRON

a reference guide

A
Reference
Publication
in
Literature

Ronald Gottesman
Editor

William
STYRON

a reference guide

JACKSON BRYER
with the assistance of
MARY BETH HATEM

G.K.HALL&CO.
70 LINCOLN STREET, BOSTON, MASS.

Copyright © 1978 by Jackson R. Bryer and
Mary Beth Hatem

Library of Congress Cataloging in Publication Data
Bryer, Jackson
  William Styron: a reference Guide

  (A reference publication in literature)
  Bibliography: p.
  Includes index
  1. Styron, William, 1925 - — Bibliography.
I. Hatem, Mary Beth, joint author
II. Series: Reference publications in literature.
Z8852.4.B78   [PS3569.T9]   016.813'5'4   78-8265
ISBN 0-8161-8042-3

This publication is printed on permanent/durable acid-free paper
MANUFACTURED IN THE UNITED STATES OF AMERICA

for Carolyn
this "man's best friend"

Contents

Introduction

It is often very difficult to bear in mind that, in a writing career which now spans more than a quarter of a century, William Styron has written only three full-length novels, a novella, a play, and a handful of reviews and essays. This relatively small body of work and its author have generated what can only be termed an extraordinary volume of critical, scholarly, and biographical commentary. Each of his three novels received well over a hundred reviews; there have been five collections of essays and reviews centered on his work; he is the sole or a primary subject of some eighteen doctoral dissertations (one of which is concerned entirely with "Sophie's Choice," Styron's current novel-in-progress); a book-length scholarly bibliography of his writings has recently been published; he has been interviewed about sixty times; and his life and work are the subject of four pamphlet-length and one full-length book. In addition, Styron's espousal of a succession of causes--from the presidential candidacy of Eugene McCarthy through his criticism of political persecution of Soviet writers down to his defense of a Connecticut teenager convicted of murdering his mother on flimsy evidence--has kept his name and opinions in the pages of American newspapers quite consistently for the past two decades. Despite all this attention, however, Styron scholarship, especially for the past eleven years, tends to be repetitive and unduly focused on The Confessions of Nat Turner and on the strong opinions and viewpoints aroused by this highly controversial novel.

William Styron never had to undergo the literary apprenticeship and gradual emergence from critical obscurity experienced by many writers. Much like F. Scott Fitzgerald, a novelist with whose works his are frequently compared, Styron became an instant critical success and literary discovery upon the publication of his first novel which in turn, with the exception of one or two pieces of juvenilia, also was his first appearance in print outside of the pages of high school or college literary magazines. When Lie Down in Darkness was published in September 1951, most reviewers hailed the 25-year-old's initial effort as remarkably precocious and a fit successor to the works of Faulkner and Wolfe. Typically, John W. Aldridge (1951.B1) saw it containing "some of the elements of greatness"; Harvey Breit (1951.B19) called it "an appallingly and terrifyingly effective (and sometimes

even moving) novel"; Maxwell Geismar (1951.B44) praised it as a "remarkable and fascinating novel--the best novel of the year by my stan-
dards--and one of the few completely human and mature novels published
since the Second World War"; Howard Mumford Jones (1951.B61) found
Styron "a craftsman of the first water"; and W. G. Rogers (1951.B99),
in a review syndicated widely throughout the country, described him
as "the most painstaking novelist, the most accomplished craftsman,
and one of the most penetrating witnesses of our life to make his debut in a decade or two." Enthusiastic praise also came from Louis D.
Rubin, Jr. (1951.B101-B102), Elizabeth Janeway (1968.B12), and Malcolm
Cowley (1951.B28), as well as from many of the book review editors of
large-city newspapers across the United States.

Those few reviewers who found fault with Lie Down in Darkness did
so usually for one of three reasons: they were shocked and outraged
by its picture of Southern life; they felt it was too long; or they
felt it was too clearly a derivative from Faulkner. An editorial in
Styron's hometown newspaper, the Newport News (Va.) Daily Press
(1951.B12), wished him well but expressed regret at "the fact that the
foundation of his popularity at present rests on the production of a
work with such a thin veneer of respectability." Ernest Cady
(1951.B25) agreed, remarking, "Surely there are more pleasant as well
as important matters which may properly engage the talents of one who
can plumb character and re-create atmosphere and put them on paper as
magnificently as William Styron does." The anonymous critic in the
Buffalo Courier-Express (1951.B4) spoke for several others when he
urged the young novelist "to learn to tighten up his prose and curb
his outpourings of poetic moodiness."

Appearing alongside the reviews in three of the major literary
periodicals, the New York Times Book Review (1951.B33), the Saturday
Review of Literature (1951.B51), and the New York Herald Tribune Book
Review (1951.B58), were interviews with Styron which further projected
him into the limelight as a literary wunderkind. The 1952 publication
of Lie Down in Darkness in Great Britain, where it was greeted polite-
ly if somewhat less enthusiastically than in the United States, a 1952
Styron interview with French critic Annie Brierre (1952.B6), and the
very favorable reception accorded Lie Down in Darkness upon its translation into French in 1953, all served to expand Styron's reputation
beyond the boundaries of his native country. In 1954, with only one
novel and a novella in print ("The Long March" had appeared in the
inaugural issue of Discovery in 1953), Styron was accorded the recognition of a Paris Review interview (1954.B3), an honor usually re-
served for more established writers. His critical respectability was
indicated also when Maxwell Geismar devoted a chapter to him in American Moderns: From Rebellion to Conformity (1958.B1).

Styron's eagerly awaited second novel, Set This House on Fire, appeared in June of 1960. Reviewers were far more divided in their appraisal of this book than they had been in evaluating Lie Down in
Darkness, perhaps because the latter had led them to expect a great

deal from Styron's new work. Time (1960.B7) dismissed it as "a 507
page crying jag"; the Virginia Quarterly Review (1960.B10) lamented
that it was "frightening to see so much talent wasted on such tawdry
material"; Donald Malcolm (1960.B76) observed sarcastically that
Styron "manages the unusual feat of stimulating the reader's curiosity
without ever arousing his interest"; and John Moreland (1960.B85) sum-
marized the objections of several other reviewers when he complained
that the new novel was "ill-constructed; its characters are hopelessly
naif and loutish; it is filled with unnecessary obscenity and scenes
which cannot even be described as debauchery, because they are so dull;
and the style is not so much 'handsome' as it is over-ornamented."
Walter Sullivan (1960.B114) made many of these same criticisms and
then noted, "Styron is no longer a beginning writer now, and in a
third novel one can hardly be content with mere promise."

But Set This House on Fire also had its supporters, many of them
prominent authors and critics. Doris Betts (1960.B14), herself a
promising young Southern novelist, hailed it as "the best thing this
reviewer has read in many years"; David Boroff (1960.B16) found it
"enthralling"; Harvey Breit considered it "an immeasurable gain in
maturity over the author's fine first novel"; Joan Didion (1960.B33)
preferred Lie Down in Darkness but added quickly that Styron "is still
running far ahead of the pack"; Granville Hicks (1960.B46) praised it
as "rich and deep" and "carefully wrought"; Robert R. Kirsch, the daily
book reviewer for the Los Angeles Times (1960.B60), described it as
"one of the finest novels I have read in a decade"; and Louis D. Rubin,
Jr. (1960.B104) saw in it "an artistry of language and a perception of
character almost unique in Mr. Styron's generation of writers."

Also in 1960, Critique, a scholarly journal focusing on post-World
War II fiction, devoted half of its Summer issue to studies of Styron's
work. Essays by Robert Gorham Davis (1960.B31), Richard Foster
(1960.B38), and David L. Stevenson (1960.B112), and a bibliography compiled by Harold W. Schneider (1960.B106) signal the beginnings of serious study of Styron by literary scholars. During the next seven years,
three or four essays or book chapters per year appeared. Chief among
these were Melvin J. Friedman's seminal introductory study of Styron's
career to date (1961.B9); Eugene McNamara's (1961.B16) and August
Nigro's (1967.B115) detailed studies of The Long March; Alice R.
Benson's critique of Set This House on Fire (1962.B7); Lewis Lawson's
Kierkegaardian reading of Lie Down in Darkness (1962.B23); important
book chapters by Robert Gorham Davis (1963.B8), Louis D. Rubin, Jr.
(1963.B22), Jonathan Baumbach (1965.B3), Robert Detweiler (1964.B5),
David Galloway (1966.B6), Louise Y. Gossett (1965.B8), and John W.
Aldridge (1966.B1); and another special issue of Critique (Winter 1965)
largely devoted to Styron, with essays by Peter L. Hays (1965.B11),
L. Hugh Moore (1965.B13), Shaun O'Connell (1965.B14), Kenneth A. Robb
(1965.B16), and Gunnar Urang (1965.B19). This period also saw the
first book publication, in 1962 in Great Britain, of The Long March
and the French translation, also in 1962, by Maurice-Edgar Coindreau,
of Set This House on Fire. This latter event, as James L. W. West III

has pointed out in the Introduction to his Styron bibliography
(1977.A2), "established Styron as a major writer in France," where it
and its author became enormously popular (see 1962.B30). Styron received further attention when he covered William Faulkner's funeral
for the July 20, 1962, issue of Life magazine and when, in 1966, he
was elected to the National Institute of Arts and Letters.

In 1967, then, William Styron was accepted as one of the major
American writers of the post-War era and as the subject of a considerable body of critical commentary. But all this previous attention
paled beside what was to follow the publication, on October 9, 1967,
of The Confessions of Nat Turner. Where critical material had previ-
ously been quite evenly directed at the full range of Styron's writings, thereafter this one novel and the often extra-literary controversies surrounding it were to dominate published criticism on its
author and to produce a scholarly redundancy which, unhappily, contin-
ues to the present time.

Lost in the memories of the harsh disagreements aroused by Nat
Turner is a fact which this Reference Guide makes clear--the great
majority of the reviews which it received were not only favorable but
also in most cases enthusiastically so. Local book critics throughout
the country praised it extravagantly and more widely recognized com-
mentators did so as well. Clifton Fadiman (1967.B48) lauded its
"extraordinary readability"; John Hope Franklin (1967.B53), one of the
few prominent blacks who liked the novel, called it "skillful and en-
grossing" and singled out Styron's "profound understanding of the in-
stitution of slavery"; Alfred Kazin (1967.B85) labelled it "a wonderfully evocative portrait"; Philip Rahv (1967.B128) saw it as "a first-
rate novel, the best that William Styron has written and the best by
an American writer that has appeared in some years"; Arthur Schlesinger,
Jr. (1967.B144) pointed appreciatively to Styron's "extraordinary perception of the subtle human admixture of strength and compassion, hate,
and self-hatred"; and Robert Coles (1968.B41) found it "a haunting and
luminous novel."

Negative responses, while much less numerous, were no less emphat-
ic. They were initiated by Herbert Aptheker who, in two early reviews
(1967.B15-B16), took Styron severely to task for his "distortion of
the historical Nat Turner." Aptheker's serious charges at first were
seconded only by Richard Greenleaf (1967.B62); but they soon were con-
siderably reinforced early in 1968 by the publication of William
Styron's Nat Turner--Ten Black Writers Respond (1968.A1), edited by
John Henrik Clarke. One of the essays in this collection, by Charles
V. Hamilton (1968.B70), had appeared before the book in the Saturday
Review and it elicited a lively exchange in the Letters to the Editors
column of that venerable journal (1968.B36). The debate was further
fueled by an exchange in the pages of The Nation between Styron himself
and Aptheker (1968.B19) and by New York Times interviews with Styron
(1968.B83) and Aptheker (1968.B18). Inevitably, the Clarke volume was
extensively reviewed and harsh appraisals of it by prominent historians

Martin Duberman (1968.B49) and Eugene Genovese (1968.B60) angered the anti-Styron forces and produced heated exchanges in the New York Times Book Review and the New York Review of Books. The final and most ironic twist of all, the awarding of the Pulitzer Prize to Nat Turner right at the height of the critical dispute over its merits, only further spurred the proponents on both sides.

As noted earlier, Nat Turner and the controversies it caused have dominated Styron criticism and scholarship since 1967. Two book-length collections have focused directly on the novel and the debate concerning its historical accuracy, Melvin J. Friedman and Irving Malin's William Styron's "The Confessions of Nat Turner"--A Critical Handbook (1970.A1) and John B. Duff and Peter M. Mitchell's The Nat Turner Rebellion: The Historical Event and the Modern Controversy (1971.A2). A proposed film version of Nat Turner reawakened the dispute about the novel's historical basis (see 1969.B3, 1969.B27, 1969.B36, 1970.B22, 1970.B24). And an alarming number of articles and book chapters over the past decade have been essentially rehashings of the Nat Turner controversy.

Amidst this regrettable redundancy, however, there have been some exceptions which can be viewed as encouraging developments--a French collection of original essays on Styron, edited by Melvin J. Friedman and August Nigro (1967.A1), which was largely ignored (probably because it appeared almost simultaneously with Nat Turner) but which contains worthwhile pieces by Nigro, David L. Stevenson, Roger Asselineau, and James Boatwright which have never been translated into English; a brief but valuable pamphlet on Styron by Richard Pearce (1971.A5) in the University of Minnesota Pamphlets on American Writers series; a longer book-length study by Marc Ratner (1972.A3) in the Twayne United States Authors series; a collection of some reprinted but mostly new essays on Styron's full career to date (including his 1972 play, "In the Clap Shack"), edited by Irving Malin and Robert K. Morris (1975.A4); and James L. W. West III's meticulously prepared and very useful bibliography of Styron's writings (1977.A2). Hopefully, this Reference Guide will add another to this relatively short list and will complement West's volume in directing attention to the full range of Styron's writing career.

This book began as "William Styron: A Bibliography," which I compiled in 1970 with Marc Newman as a contribution to Friedman and Malin's Critical Handbook on Nat Turner (1970.A1). Lewis Lawson and Susan Robinson were of considerable assistance in the preparation of that listing. A later compilation, which was primarily an updating, appeared in Malin and Morris's The Achievement of William Styron (1975.A4). Joanne Giza helped in the preparation of that version. The present volume represents an annotating of all items in the earlier two checklists, an updating of the 1975 version; but, most significantly, it adds many new entries to both earlier listings. The major source of these additions was the Styron Collection at the Perkins Library of Duke University. I am grateful to James L. W. West III for

alerting me to the riches of the Duke holdings (and for innumerable
other acts of scholarly generosity) and to Mattie M. Russell, Curator
of Manuscripts, for being so genial and helpful during my two visits
to Durham. William Styron generously allowed me to see the scrapbooks
of clippings kept by his father and deposited in Duke's collection.
For significant help in locating and verifying material, I thank Jane
De Mouy and Ruth M. Alvarez and the many reference librarians throughout the world who answered my letters. Without the aid of these anonymous correspondents, my work would have been impossible.

This Reference Guide attempts to list all the criticism and commentary on Styron in English which I could locate. The listing of
reviews of English editions of Styron's novel is incomplete because I
simply could not find and verify some of the references. I have made
only a token effort to include foreign pieces on Styron and, outside
of the interviews in foreign languages, I have not annotated the foreign items which I have included. Styron's reputation abroad, especially in France, could well be the subject of another volume. The
files at Duke contain many clippings in foreign languages, most partic-
ularly French reviews of Set This House on Fire and Nat Turner, and
the interested researcher is advised to consult these for further material of this sort. In general, I have adhered to the style of earlier Reference Guides, with one small eccentricity: for general essays
or reviews which contain only brief mention of Styron, the pages of the
full piece are listed first, with the pages on Styron following in
brackets. Occasionally, I have relied on listings in the West bibliography (1977.A2) in annotating foreign interviews or in citing foreign
references. In addition, essays or public letters which are responses
to or which elicited responses from Styron are cross-indexed to appro-
priate entries in West.

Writings about
William Styron, 1946-1978

1946 A BOOKS - NONE

1946 B SHORTER WRITINGS

   1   MATCH, RICHARD. "Duke Student Verse," New York Herald Tribune
       Weekly Book Review (3 February), p. 16.
           Review of One and Twenty: Duke Narrative and Verse,
       1924-1946, in which Styron's contribution, "Autumn," is men-
       tioned very briefly.

1951 A BOOKS - NONE

1951 B SHORTER WRITINGS

   1   ALDRIDGE, JOHN W. "In a Place Where Love Is a Stranger," New
       York Times Book Review (9 September), p. 5.
           Lie Down in Darkness is a "first novel containing some
       of the elements of greatness, one with which the work of no
       other young writer of 25 can be compared."

   2   ANON. Pre-publication Review of Lie Down in Darkness, Retail
       Bookseller, 54 (September), 104.
           Reviewer suggests that Peyton is "a sort of F. Scott
       Fitzgerald character."

   3   ANON. "Facts and Fiction--Some Virginia Scenes and Situations
       as Viewed By Novelist," Norfolk Virginian-Pilot (9 Septem-
       ber), Part 5, p. 5.
           Localities and situations in Lie Down in Darkness which
       would be recognizable to Virginians are described.

   4   ANON. Review of Lie Down in Darkness, Buffalo Courier-Express
       (9 September), p. 22-D.
           Styron is "undeniably the most interesting and promising
       young novelist to come along in several years." But, tech-
       nically, "he still needs to learn to tighten up his prose
       and curb his outpourings of poetic moodiness."

1951

5   ANON. "Dark Misery," <u>Newsweek</u>, 38 (10 September), 106-107.
    "When the intensity of his story drops, it collapses...."

6   ANON. "The Unbeautiful and Damned," <u>Time</u>, 58 (10 September),
    106, 108.
        "Author Styron leaves his unbeautiful people in the rhet-
    oric of tragedy, but essentially they remain moral pygmies."

7   ANON. "'Pathetic' Characters in Today's Literature," Durham
    (N.C.) <u>Morning Herald</u> (14 September), Sec. 1, p. 4.
        An editorial which agrees with Orville Prescott (1951.B92)
    that Styron's characters in <u>Lie Down in Darkness</u> are pathet-
    ic rather than tragic.

8   ANON. "Books New and Noticeable," Cleveland <u>Plain Dealer</u> (16
    September), p. 33-D.
        Brief U.P.I. syndicated review of <u>Lie Down in Darkness</u>:
    "a convincing novel that would do credit to a Thomas Wolfe."

9   ANON. Review of <u>Lie Down in Darkness</u>, <u>New Yorker</u>, 27 (29 Sep-
    tember), 118-19.
        Styron "has made the coffin too big for what is, when
    all is said and done, only a very young, slight over-wrought
    body."

10 ANON. "Books," <u>Duke University Alumni Register</u>, 37 (October),
    251.
        An account of the composition of <u>Lie Down in Darkness</u>
    and a brief biographical sketch of its author.

11 ANON. "Local Author Important, W & M Professor Says," Newport
    News (Va.) <u>Daily Press</u> (16 November), p. 2.
        A report of a lecture on Styron given by Dr. G. Glenwood
    Clark to the Women's Club of Fort Monroe, Virginia.

12 ANON. "'Lie Down in Darkness,'" Newport News (Va.) <u>Daily Press</u>
    (23 November), p. 4.
        Editorial in Styron's hometown newspaper. "We wish Bill
    Styron every success as a writer but are saddened by the
    fact that the foundation of his popularity at present rests
    on the production of a work with such a thin veneer of re-
    spectability. Let us hope he bases his next on something
    more lasting."

13 AULT, PHIL. "The Parents' Sins," Los Angeles <u>Mirror</u> (21 Sep-
    tember), p. 30.
        Although Styron "is not yet a great novelist," <u>Lie Down
    in Darkness</u> shows him to have "the depth, imagination and

ability to express ideas that well may elevate him someday
to the literary top."

14   BALE, JOY. "Into the Dark of the Heart," Louisville <u>Courier-
     Journal</u> (16 September), Sec. 3, p. 10.
     "Few contemporary writers have succeeded as well as
     William Styron in sustaining a depressive atmosphere which
     becomes subordinate to the larger purpose of his characters.
     If the test of serious fiction is the enlarging of man's
     understanding of man, 'Lie Down in Darkness' meets the test
     most ably."

15   BEDELL, W. D. "William Styron--Bitter Story Hits Home,"
     Houston <u>Post</u> (9 September), Sec. 1, p. 22.
     <u>Lie Down in Darkness</u> is a "tragedy of American life that,
     while definitely exaggerated, is one of the truest to be
     written in decades."

16   BELL, BLAKE KENNEDY. "Gifted New Pen Is Indigo-Dipped--William
     Styron's First Novel Shows Talent," Tulsa <u>Daily World</u> (23
     September), Sec. 5, p. 9.
     <u>Lie Down in Darkness</u> is "a wonderfully well-written book,
     very possibly by a new master. For those who bleed with
     believable characters (the reviewer does, and all Styron's
     are) the gore will constitute a near hemorrhage."

17   BLACKMAN, EUGENE J. Review of <u>Lie Down in Darkness</u>, Boston
     <u>Sunday Post</u> (16 September), p. 52.
     <u>Lie Down in Darkness</u> is "a brilliant masterpiece of lit-
     erary form, possessing haunting beauty and evoking in the
     reader feelings of admiration and excitement."

18   BREEN, MELWYN. "Southern Bloom in Dust," <u>Saturday Night</u>
     (Toronto), 67 (27 October), 22.
     Although Styron is young, in <u>Lie Down in Darkness</u>, "the
     grasp he has of his subject and the poetic and perceptive
     presentation of it make him ageless."

19   BREIT, HARVEY. "Dissolution of a Family," <u>Atlantic Monthly</u>,
     188 (October), 78-80.
     <u>Lie Down in Darkness</u> is "an appallingly and terrifyingly
     effective (and sometimes even moving) novel."

20   B[ROADDUS], M[ARIAN] H[OWE]. "Glancing Through the New Books
     With Marian Howe Broaddus," El Paso <u>Times</u> (16 September),
     p. 8.
     "Mr. Styron writes well, and with patient and thoughtful

1951

finesse, but his persistence in viewing the world through a glass, darkly, is a bit dispiriting."

21 BROWN, ALEXANDER C. "Lie Down In Darkness--A Review," Newport News (Va.) Daily Press (9 September), p. 4-D.
"I feel like a prissy spinster for saying that it is a pity he did not write about somebody nice. But it is just that. It seems a waste of talent and on occasion the writer himself becomes ensnared in his own web of gloom."

22 BULLOCK, DICK. "Southern Locale," Charleston (S.C.) News and Courier (16 September), Sec. C, p. 1.
Lie Down in Darkness is "an unusually fine first novel from a twenty-six year old writer with a very promising talent."

23 BYAM, MILTON S. Review of Lie Down in Darkness, Library Journal, 76 (15 September), 1423-24.
"It has the solid ring of tragedy that will gnaw, like the corruption it paints, at the hearts of one and all."

24 C., H. B. "Family Which Destroys Itself," Worcester Sunday Telegram (9 September), Sec. B, p. 11.
Lie Down in Darkness demonstrates that Styron's "talent is not yet ripe enough to portray sickness of soul without descending to theatricalism and tawdriness nor to describe the loneliness of modern youth...without becoming tiresome by indulging in repetitious hysteria."

25 C[ADY], E[RNEST]. "Impressive First Novel Surmounts Handicap of Overworked Theme," Columbus (Ohio) Sunday Dispatch (9 September), p. F-7.
"Surely there are more pleasant as well as important matters which may properly engage the talents of one who can plumb character and re-create atmosphere and put them on paper as magnificently as William Styron does.

26 CARTER, RUTH S. "Depth and Power Found in 'Lie Down in Darkness,'" Houston Chronicle (9 September), p. E 5.
In Lie Down in Darkness, Styron "displays a depth and sureness of insight unusual in beginning writers; his material is interesting, well-organized, and full of the emotional ramifications that build up compelling stories."

27 CHAPIN, RUTH. "Twilight of the South," Christian Science Monitor (4 October), p. 11.
"Among the writers Styron has tasted and--to his credit--

very nearly digested are Thomas Wolfe, James Joyce and William Faulkner."

28   COWLEY, MALCOLM. "The Faulkner Pattern," New Republic, 125 (8 October), 19-20.
     "It is a general rule that novels which stay close to their literary models have no great value of their own, but Lie Down in Darkness is an exception; in this case the example of Faulkner seems to have had a liberating effect on Styron's imagination."

29   CROSS, LESLIE. "The Reading Glass," Milwaukee Journal (16 September), Editorial Section, p. 5.
     Brief biographical sketch of Styron.

30   CRUME, PAUL. "Strong Novel of Virginia Tragedy," Dallas Morning News (9 September), Part VI, p. 7.
     "The touch of talent is everywhere about" Lie Down in Darkness.

31   DAVIS, RICHARD. "Debt Acknowledged," Little Rock Gazette (11 November), p. 6F.
     Largely descriptive review of Lie Down in Darkness, with considerable comparison of Styron and Faulkner.

32   DAVIS, ROBERT GORHAM. "A Grasp of Moral Realities," American Scholar, 21 (Winter), 114, 116.
     "William Styron has dazzling gifts with language, and great observational powers in describing moods, incidents, landscapes and conversations. But it is the moral tension of his best scenes that gives such dramatic interest to a story which in outline is so familiarly depressing...."

33   DEMPSEY, DAVID. "Talk With William Styron," New York Times Book Review (9 September), p. 27.
     Interview in which William Styron talks about Lie Down in Darkness, refusing to call his writing "Southern," and comments on those writers who have influenced his work—Faulkner, Joyce, and Twain.

34   DERLETH, AUGUST. "Idea Is Good But It Needs a Little Editing." Chicago Sunday Tribune Magazine of Books (9 September), p. 3.
     "Wisdom and compassion are surely here; much insight and perception flash thru its pages; but Mr. Styron leaves his readers curiously unsympathetic."

1951

35 DONNELLY, TOM. "We Need a Few Hard Superlatives Around Here,"
    Washington (D.C.) Daily News (7 September), p. 37.
        In Lie Down in Darkness, Styron shows that he has "con-
    siderable technical skill," fine description, and "believ-
    able" characters; but he relies on a melodramatic plot,
    which, though it reflects contemporary failures, "is not a
    portrait of our times." Nonetheless, the novel is "a re-
    spectable achievement."

36 DOWNING, FRANCIS. "The Young: A Lost Generation," Commonweal,
    54 (5 October), 619-20.
        Reviewer warns that, as Peyton Loftis suggests, "we will
    lose the younger generation by empty preaching."

37 DWIGHT, OGDEN G. "Year's Third New Major Writer, Styron,
    Hailed For Brilliant Novel," Des Moines Sunday Register (9
    September), p. 11-W.
        Lie Down in Darkness "exhibits an insight, style and
    command of language which are little short of astonishing"
    and is "a book, a real book, by a writer of first importance
    who has something important to say."

38 E[ARL], L[EONARD] F[RANCIS]. "Depressing Family Tale," Win-
    nipeg (Manitoba) Tribune (20 October), p. 13.
        Lie Down in Darkness is "a piece of exceptional writing."

39 ELWOOD, IRENE. "Family Has Everything, Loses All," Los Angeles
    Times (16 September), Sec. 4, p. 5.
        Lie Down in Darkness misses "the hard, clean core of
    tragedy"; but it "may be enjoyed for its distinctive style."

40 FARBER, JAMES. "Parade of Books," New York Journal American,
    (29 September), p. 8. This syndicated review also appeared
    in Baltimore News Post (29 September); Seattle Intelligencer
    (29 September); Milwaukee Sentinel (29 September); Albany
    (N.Y.) Times-Union (30 September).
        "After gluing yourself to this prosy piece of stream-of-
    consciousness for the requisite number of hours, you may
    wonder what, indeed, you have gotten out of it. I daresay
    the answer won't be soul-stirring, but you will have at
    least been quite absorbed by the monumental foolishness of
    it all."

41 FOWLER, ROBERT. "Virginian Writes Lucid Prose," Greensboro
    (N.C.) Daily News (9 September), Feature Section, p. 3.
        In Lie Down in Darkness, Styron "writes with a Faulknerian
    flow, but still manages a degree of clarity which would

enhance his senior's tales of corn cobs and Deep Southern
decadence."

42   GANNETT, LEWIS. "Books and Things," New York Herald Tribune
      (11 September), p. 25.
           Although the "unique and macabre structure" of Lie Down
      in Darkness is "a technical achievement of rare virtuosity,"
      it "takes more than technical skill to make a great novel,
      and some readers...may wonder whether Mr. Styron, for all
      his vivid words, really understands the 'human heart in
      conflict with itself' which is said to be his major theme."

43   GARDNER, R. H. "A Promising First Novel and Another," Baltimore
      Evening Sun (25 October), p. 30.
           Lie Down in Darkness shows that "Mr. Styron is an unques-
      tionably competent craftsman. The net effect of his work
      might have been greater had he not been so preoccupied with
      dissecting each minute emotional detail. Even so, his power
      cannot be denied."

44   GEISMAR, MAXWELL. "Domestic Tragedy in Virginia," Saturday
      Review of Literature, 34 (15 September), 12-13.
           Lie Down in Darkness is a "remarkable and fascinating
      novel--the best novel of the year by my standards--and one
      of the few completely human and mature novels published
      since the Second World War."

45   GOULD, JOHN. "Frank Appraisals of Latest Books," Wichita Falls
      (Texas) Times (14 October), p. 9D.
           "For all its uncheerfulness," Lie Down in Darkness is
      "a surprisingly well-written story."

46   GOULD, RAY. "Astonishing First Novel Is Brilliant," Montgomery
      (Ala.) Advertiser (4 November), p. 9-D.
           Lie Down in Darkness is "an extraordinary novel devised
      and written by a new writer with worlds of talent."

47   GOVAN, CHRISTINE NOBLE. "Story of Weak Family Is Plea For
      More Maturity in Adults," Chattanooga Times (16 September),
      p. 19.
           In Lie Down in Darkness, Styron's "consuming pity, his
      anger and his fervor are always under leash and therefore
      effective." He has "something of the flame that is found
      in Wolfe and Faulkner."

48   G[REENING], M[ARJORIE] M. "About Books....," Michigan City
      (Ind.) News-Dispatch (4 October), p. 10.

7

1951

> *Lie Down in Darkness* is "a truly outstanding first
> novel."

49 GROVE, LEE. "Memorable First Novel Demolishes a Family,"
    Washington *Post* (9 September), p. 6-B.
    "The grasp of character and development of action [in
    Lie Down in Darkness] would be a credit to a writer of any
    age, and considering Styron's youth, they are indications
    of great talent."

50 HANSEN, HARRY. "Beginning of a Novelist: Releasing Toy Bal-
    loons," *Chicago Sunday Tribune Magazine of Books* (23 Sep-
    tember), p. 12.
    Biographical sketch of Styron and a brief description of
    the literary influences reflected in *Lie Down in Darkness*.

51 HARRISON, KATHARINE. "Critics Laud Styron Style; New Novel
    Comes Off Press," Newport News (Va.) *Daily Press* (9 Septem-
    ber), p. 14-C.
    Excerpts from reviews of *Lie Down in Darkness* and a de-
    tailed biographical sketch of Styron, with emphasis on his
    Newport News background.

52 H[AZARD], E[LOISE] P[ERRY]. "The Author," *Saturday Review of
    Literature*, 34 (15 September), 12.
    A biographical note on Styron, featuring quotes from
    Styron on his start as a writer and on the composition of
    Lie Down in Darkness.

53 HETH, EDWARD HARRIS. "A Torrential New Talent," Milwaukee
    Journal (16 September), Sec. 5, p. 5.
    It is evident from reading *Lie Down in Darkness* that
    Styron "has an emotional and artistic quality that seems to
    have died in many older American writers."

54 HILL, BOB. "Looking at Books," Spokane (Wash.) *Chronicle* (13
    September), p. 32.
    Lie Down in Darkness is "a book vast and complicated in
    design and rich, as few contemporary novels are, in emotion-
    al texture....it's a fine and memorable novel, at times
    very nearly a great one."

55 HORAN, KENNETH. "Willa Cather's World; Two Problem Novels,"
    Dallas *Times-Herald* (16 September), Sec. 8, p. 3.
    In *Lie Down in Darkness* is "the sadness of life all
    wrapped up in a package of gloom."

56   HOYT, ELIZABETH NORTH. "Disintegration," Cedar Rapids (Iowa)
      Gazette (7 October), Sec. 3, p. 8.
          In Lie Down in Darkness, the "echo of past masters is
      faint and Mr. Styron has designed and built a story that is
      a tour de force in its own right."

57   HUNT, HOWARD. "Evil Likewise Begins at Home In New Novel,"
      San Antonio Express (16 September), p. 4 D.
          "Although only 26, Styron displays mature wisdom and in-
      sight hardly to be expected from a man of his few years."

58   HUTCHENS, JOHN K. "On the Books--On an Author," New York
      Herald Tribune Book Review (9 September), p. 2.
          Biographical sketch of Styron and discussion of Lie
      Down in Darkness, with emphasis on strong influence of
      Faulkner on Styron's style in his first novel.

59   JOHNSON, STANLEY. "Again the Decay of an Old Southern Family--
      This Time With Success," Salt Lake Tribune (14 October),
      Magazine, p. 4M.
          Lie Down in Darkness "plunges so deeply into the problems
      of character motivation, it throws such a searching light
      on human behavior, it creates such painfully believable
      characters, that it conveys the impression that a portion
      of life is being seen and understood for the first time."

60   JONES, CARTER BROOKE. "Work of Virginia's William Styron
      Hailed as Extraordinary First Novel," Washington (D.C.)
      Sunday Star (9 September), p. 3-C.
          Lie Down in Darkness is "such a mature and penetrating
      record of a family, written with such unerring skill, that
      it deserves to establish the author, regardless of whether
      he ever publishes another line."

61   JONES, HOWARD MUMFORD. "A Rich, Moving Novel Introduces a
      Young Writer of Great Talent," New York Herald Tribune Book
      Review (9 September), p. 3.
          "Despite its echoes of familiar authors, Lie Down in
      Darkness is satisfying work." Styron has "fertility of
      invention, he knows how to manage a long novel, and in the
      economy of his tale he proves himself a craftsman of the
      first water."

62   KELLEY, JAMES E. "Promising First Novel--Violence of Love and
      Hate," Denver Post (9 September), p. 6E.
          Lie Down in Darkness "deserves a place on the shelf re-
      served for the most promising literary talents of the year."

1951

63 KIMMEL, L. F. "Eagle Eye on Books," Wichita <u>Eagle</u> (19 September), p. 6.
    Styron "knows how to delve into human hearts and accurately analyze human reactions."

64 LANING, CLAIR. "Books and People..," Oakville (Ontario) <u>Record-Star</u> (11 October).
    Styron "is a good writer even if his book does not live up to the publisher's ballyhoo." This unverified clipping was seen at the Duke University Library.

65 L[AYCOCK], E[DWARD] A. "An Exciting Discovery--William Styron Writes Magnificent First Novel About a Tragic Family," Boston <u>Sunday Globe</u> (9 September), p. 27-A.
    "The story will shock you at times, but it will move you deeply."

66 LERNER, MAX. "The Generations," New York <u>Post</u> (17 September), p. 24.
    Consideration of <u>Lie Down in Darkness</u>--"It's a bit over-literary, and there are echoes in it of Faulkner and Wolfe, but the fellow can write like an angel."--as a point of departure for remarks on parent-child relationships.

67 M., M. Review of <u>Lie Down in Darkness</u>, Kingston (Ontario) <u>Whig-Standard</u> (22 December), p. 4.
    <u>Lie Down in Darkness</u> is "a most remarkable book, full of insight, skillful writing and powerful descriptions."

68 MacGREGOR, MARTHA. "Impressive First Novel By a Talented 26-Year-Old Writer," New York <u>Post</u> (9 September), p. 12M.
    "What makes this novel outstanding and important are the people....They are human beings living their lives and an impressive creative achievement."

69 McGRORY, MARY. "Reading and Writing--Hard-Boiled Marines Realize Claims of Literature, Defer Reservist Writer," Washington (D.C.) <u>Sunday Star</u> (5 August), p. C-3.
    Account of how U.S. Marine Corps gave Styron two-month deferment at request of his publisher so that he could finish <u>Lie Down in Darkness</u>.

70 McHUGH, MIRIAM. "Today's Books," Trenton (N.J.) <u>Trentonian</u> (22 September), p. 13.
    "The Loftis picture is candid enough but Styron would have done better by merely telling their story instead of attempting to picture the cast as victims of today's decay."

71   MacLAREN, HALE. "Looks at Books," La Jolla (Calif.) Light (27
      December), p. 3-B.
            "The most appalling aspect [of Lie Down in Darkness] is
      the fact that here is a novel, well-written and in its tor-
      tuous way well-conceived, which gives only despair to the
      reading public."

72   MASON, ROBERT. "Story of the Spirit Is Rich in Poetry and
      Insight--William Styron of Newport News, 26, Is Suddenly a
      Major Novelist," Norfolk Virginian-Pilot (9 September),
      Part 5, p. 4.
            "As a craftsman and artist, William Styron at the age of
      26 bears risk of the word genius."

73   _____. "Teacher Guided, Publisher Fired Him--Encouragement
      and a Kick Made Bill Styron a Writer," Norfolk Virginian-
      Pilot (9 September), Part 5, p. 5.
            Detailed biographical sketch based on an interview with
      Styron's father which focuses on his son's decision to be-
      come a writer.

74   MELTON, AMOS. "Fine Talent Is Misused In 1st Novel," Fort
      Worth Star-Telegram (23 September), Sec. 2, p. 11.
            In Lie Down in Darkness, Styron "handles his people and
      situations well. He has a fine skill. However, one can
      not but wonder what the result would be if such fine talent
      were turned toward a newer section and a brighter faith."

75   MORGAN-POWELL, S. "Some New Novels--English and American
      Tales Provide a Striking Contrast," Montreal Star (20 Octo-
      ber), p. 20.
            Lie Down in Darkness "is remarkable more for its fine
      analytical qualities and its beauty of writing than for any
      originality in plot."

76   MORRISSY, W. B. "Disintegration of a Family," Montreal Gazette
      (27 October), p. 27.
            In Lie Down in Darkness, Styron writes "with power and
      passion and an almost incredible insight for a stripling of
      26."

77   MORTON, JOSEPH J. Review of Lie Down in Darkness, Brooklyn
      Eagle (16 September), p. 27.
            In Lie Down in Darkness, Styron "has a deep insight into
      the problems and tragedy of life, but has neglected to add
      the alieviating comic touches which lend such sparkle to
      the work of" Truman Capote and Speed Lamkin; but "the

1951

> problem dealt with by Mr. Styron has a qualifying universal-
> ity that removes it from the class of regional fiction."

78   MOSSMAN, JOSEF. "Horrid Limbo of Lost Souls," Detroit <u>News</u>
       (23 September), Home and Society Section, p. 17.
       "While young Mr. Styron is undeniably a talented writer,
       he is not yet the omniscient authority on humanity and eter-
       nity that he should have been to undertake so portentous
       and significant a theme. It is only fair to record, how-
       ever, that he shows every promise of becoming so."

79   MUNN, L. S. "Mature Young Talent Seen In 'Lie Down in Dark-
       ness,'" Springfield (Mass.) <u>Sunday Republican</u> (30 September),
       p. 10B.
       <u>Lie Down in Darkness</u> is "a remarkable novel, not by any
       standards a 'promising' novel, for it attains its own com-
       manding stature in conception and execution by a writer
       whose youth is immaterial since he possesses the ability to
       delve adroitly and searchingly into the shabby souls of his
       intellectual creations."

80   NELSON, NORMAN K. "Personality of the Week--Bill Styron of
       Duke Called Second Wolfe," Charlotte <u>Observer</u> (23 September),
       p. 12-D. This article also appeared in Asheville (N.C.)
       <u>Citizen</u> (23 September).
       Detailed biographical sketch and praise for <u>Lie Down in
       Darkness</u>.

81   NICHOLSON, HENRY. "Unhappiness Dissected," Rochester (N.Y.)
       <u>Democrat and Chronicle</u> (30 September), p. 10D.
       In <u>Lie Down in Darkness</u>, Styron is "proficient in evoking
       'atmosphere' in conventional descriptive prose and also in
       passages whose purpose is to establish an abstract mood."

82   NORTH, STERLING. "Sterling North Reviews the New Books--An
       Important First Novel," New York <u>World Telegram</u> (11 Septem-
       ber), p. 26. This review also appeared in Toledo <u>Blade</u> (30
       September).
       Styron is "good enough to warrant (and important enough
       to deserve) objective criticism. Meanwhile, those who miss
       his novel are missing an experience."

83   O'BRIEN, ALFRED, JR. "<u>Lie Down in Darkness</u>," <u>Commonweal</u>, 55
       (19 October), 43-44.
       Largely descriptive review which sees Peyton as a modern
       prodigal son.

84 O'CONNOR, RICHARD. "Lie Down in Darkness," Los Angeles Herald
    Express (22 September), Sec. A, p. 12.
        Although Styron has still to learn to "edit himself," he
    has "the ability to penetrate to the vital core of his char-
    acters, often with an economy of language, a flash of the
    scalpel, that compels respect and a great hope for his
    future."

85 O'DELL, SCOTT. "New Novelist Makes Auspicious Debut," Los
    Angeles Daily News (15 September), p. 8.
        Although Styron's "people are too special, too morally
    mean, to either enlist the reader's sympathies or to bring
    off the tragic implications" which he intends, he has "an
    elastic prose," "knowledge, beyond his years, of middle-
    aged motives," "a surging, tireless power of expression,
    and an uncommon technical skill."

86 O'LEARY, THEODORE M. "Styron's Remarkable First Novel,"
    Kansas City Star (29 September), p. 16.
        Lie Down in Darkness "dramatizes human agony with unusual
    clarity and compassion."

87 OLIVER, JOAN. "Bill Styron," The Archive (Duke University),
    65 (Fall), 18-19.
        Detailed biographical sketch.

88 P., A. F. "Wealth Does Not Bring Happiness," Hamilton (Ontario)
    Spectator (27 October), p. 16.
        Basically descriptive review of Lie Down in Darkness.

89 PACE, NORMA W. "Lie Down in Darkness, A Puzzler," Lexington
    (Ky.) Herald-Leader (23 September), p. 23.
        Lie Down in Darkness is a "powerful volume"; but "a
    writer who concerns himself with only sex, religion and
    death is not giving a true picture, no matter how effec-
    tive nor how convincing his finished work may be."

90 PARKE, MARY EUGENIA. "Facts and Fiction--Critics of Styron's
    Novel Agree Only on His Talent," Norfolk Virginian-Pilot
    (7 October), Part 5, p. 5.
        Summaries of reviews of Lie Down in Darkness organized
    around the several major schools of thought about it.

91 PASLEY, GERTRUDE. "Unhappy People," Newark (N.J.) Sunday News
    (16 September), Sec. 4, p. 88.
        "Despite its morbidity," Lie Down in Darkness is "ex-
    tremely well written."

13

1951

92 PRESCOTT, ORVILLE. "Books of The Times," New York <u>Times</u> (10 September), p. 19.
    <u>Lie Down in Darkness</u> represents "such an explosive combination of blazing power and exasperating confusion of thought and narrative that it should stir up a fine controversy."

93 PRICE, EMERSON. "Hails Young Author's First Novel," Cleveland <u>Press</u> (11 September), p. 18.
    <u>Lie Down in Darkness</u> "is tragedy, this book, fully and magnificently realized--the great tragedy of our own times. But there is also an element of faith which each reader must find for himself."

94 RAGAN, MARJORIE. "A New Southern Author Shows Literary Promise," Raleigh <u>News and Observer</u> (16 September), Sec. 4, p. 5.
    "Those who want an engrossing story of fine form and style will want this book."

95 RAGAN, SAM. "Southern Accent," Raleigh <u>News and Observer</u> (16 September), Sec. 4, p. 5.
    Biographical note on Styron and discussion of the healthy critical reception of <u>Lie Down in Darkness</u>.

96 ROBINSON, FRANCES. Review of <u>Lie Down in Darkness</u>, <u>Book-of-the-Month Club News</u> (September), p. 14.
    Despite Styron's "tendency to overwrite, he makes his effect in this first novel and reveals himself as a writer who may be disliked or disagreed with but is not likely to be ignored."

97 R[OBINSON], O[LIVE] C. "<u>Lie Down in Darkness</u>," Lewiston (Me.) <u>Sun</u> (13 September), p. 4.
    <u>Lie Down in Darkness</u> "is essentially art for art's sake and it is probable that the book will have its widest reading among the intellectual sophisticates."

98 ROCKWELL, KENNETH. "First Novel Introduces Major Literary Talent," Dallas <u>Times-Herald</u> (9 September), Sec. 7, p. 3.
    "How so young a man could produce <u>Lie Down in Darkness</u> is a puzzle to be worked out by those psychologists who attempt to understand the ways of genius."

99 R[OGERS], W. G. "First Novel 'Remarkable,'" Omaha <u>Sunday World Herald</u> (16 September), p. 28-G. This syndicated review also appeared in Trenton (N.J.) <u>Times</u> (30 September); Manchester (N.H.) <u>News</u> (9 September); Scranton (Penna.)

14

<u>Tribune</u> (14 October); San Mateo (Calif.) <u>Times</u> (11 September); Keene (N.H.) <u>Sentinel</u> (13 September); Woonsocket (R.I.) <u>Call</u> (27 September); Binghamton (N.Y.) <u>Press</u> (9 September); Phoenix <u>Gazette</u> (11 September); Aberdeen (Wash.) <u>World</u> (12 September); Bakersfield (Calif.) <u>Californian</u> (11 September).

Styron has "uncommon gifts" and is "the most painstaking novelist, the most accomplished craftsman, and one of the most penetrating witnesses of our life to make his debut in a decade or two."

100 ROTHERMEL, J. F. "Needed--A Good Editor--A Tragic Story Involving Twisted People and Told With Powerful Writing," Birmingham (Ala.) <u>News</u> (9 September), Sec. F, p. 6.

Styron has "an adolescent conviction all life is dark with only light spots to heighten the tragedy. If he could reverse his chiaroscuro, reading him would be more pleasant, but his writing would not necessarily be any better."

101 RUBIN, LOUIS D., JR. "Two Significant Southern Novels Point to Importance of Religious Faith in Society," Richmond (Va.) <u>News Leader</u> (10 September), p. 11.

"The total effect of <u>Lie Down in Darkness</u> is a successful one--in a sense, the very haze at the beginning contributes to the mood of aimless longing and purposelessness. Mr. Styron is obviously a man with much to say, and the literary wherewithal to say it well."

102 _____. "What To Do About Chaos," <u>Hopkins Review</u>, 5 (Fall), 65-68.

<u>Lie Down in Darkness</u> is "an excellently contrived, successfully executed novel."

103 S., F. G. Review of <u>Lie Down in Darkness</u>, South Bend (Ind.) <u>Tribune</u> (18 October), Sec. 1, p. 8.

"Styron has made a remarkable start and no doubt will win attention. His next novel should be something much better, finer and, let us hope, with a more wholesome subject."

104 SCOTT, ELEANOR M. Review of <u>Lie Down in Darkness</u>, Providence <u>Sunday Journal</u> (9 September), Sec. 6, p. 8.

"The reader wonders what the author's next novel will be like while at the same time doubting whether this one should have been published."

105 SESSLER, BETTY. Review of <u>Lie Down in Darkness</u>, Richmond (Va.) <u>Times-Dispatch</u> (16 September), p. 8-A.

1951

"Styron writes with feeling and understanding. What he lacks is organization and concentration."

106 SHERMAN, JOHN K. "First Novel Stamps Young Writer as Great," Minneapolis Sunday Tribune (30 September), Feature-News Section, p. 6.

    Styron is "already possessed of deep perception, an authentic sense of the tragic, an unfailing artistry of prose, and ruthless penetration of motives, open and hidden."

107 SMITH, HARRISON. "Young Writer Depicts Trials of Human Soul," Buffalo Evening News (8 September), Magazine, p. 7. This syndicated review also appeared in Charlotte Observer (9 September); Philadelphia Sunday Bulletin (9 September); Easton (Penna.) Express (8 September); Roanoke Times (9 September); Youngstown Vindicator (9 September); Hartford Times (8 September); Brattleboro (Vt.) Reformer (5 September); San Diego Union (9 September).

    Despite its themes, Lie Down in Darkness "does not have the quality of hopelessness in humanity so common in the novels of other young writers today."

108 SNYDER, MARJORIE B. "Love, Hate, Passion All in His Book," Boston Sunday Herald (9 September), Sec. 1, p. 6.

    Lie Down in Darkness is "compassionate, but not mawkish, and is as vital as a heartbeat." Styron is a new "major talent."

109 [SPECTORSKY, A. C.] "Worth Reading," Charm, 75 (October), 30.

    Lie Down in Darkness is "one of the most moving and revealing portraits of a tormented young woman's mind and emotions that has yet been written."

110 STIX, FREDERICK W. Review of Lie Down in Darkness, Cincinnati Enquirer (9 September), Sec. 3, p. 13.

    Styron is a "new and interesting young writer"; but "the reader will wonder whether Sytron has chosen worthy material."

111 SULLIVAN, JULIAN T. "Decay and Death Fertilize Fine New Creative Talent," Indianapolis Star (16 September), Sec. 6, p. 14.

    Lie Down in Darkness gives "resounding force" to the old theme of the degeneracy of a Southern family. His artistic maturity and the completeness of his pessimistic philosphy leave the reader intellectually excited and emotionally saturated, but wondering if Styron believes "in the possibility of happiness."

112   SWADOS, HARVEY. "First Novel," The Nation, 272 (24 November),
       453.
            "The undeniable phosphorescent glow of books like Mr.
       Styron's is utterly sufficient without an original under-
       standing of the world in which the characters move--and
       this is precisely what is missing in Mr. Styron's otherwise
       noteworthy first novel."

113   TONEY, SARA D. "The Mariners Bookstall," Gloucester (Mass.)
       Daily Times (3 October), p. 9.
            Although the flashbacks are "somewhat annoying," Lie
       Down in Darkness "has been done with infinite care."

114   TRUAX, CHARLES. "New Novel of Family's Tragedy Hailed,"
       Dayton Daily News (16 September), Sec. 2, p. 9.
            Lie Down in Darkness "treats of ugliness and corruption,
       yet it is neither ugly nor corrupt itself. It comes very
       close to being a great novel; certainly its author, at age
       26, emerges as one of the most promising literary crafts-
       men in many years."

115   TURNER, E.S. "'Lie Down in Darkness' Reveals a New Talent,"
       Syracuse Herald (16 September), Features Section, p. 37.
            "The Loftises are not representative or typical of any
       but their own miniscule strain in the millions of tough-
       fibred, clean-living families in America." But Lie Down in
       Darkness is "a work of art."

116   WALLACE, MARGARET. "Of a Nobel Laureate and Other Novelists,"
       Independent Woman, 30 (November), 325.
            Lie Down in Darkness ranks Styron "as a member, and by
       no means the least considerable member, of that distin-
       guished group of Southern writers whose names are generally
       headed by Faulkner and Wolfe."

117   WEEKS, MABEL. "First Novel Shoots Straight to Heart," Long
       Beach (Calif.) Press-Telegram (9 September), Southland Mag-
       azine, p. 13.
            Lie Down in Darkness "seems destined to have universal
       appeal."

118   WINN, ELIZABETH S. "The Bookshelf," El Paso Herald-Post (20
       October), p. 4.
            "Such excesses" as Styron indulges in, "from a literary
       point of view, are easily forgiven because of the apparent
       sincerity and intensity of the prose."

1951

119   WYNNE, LESLIE B. "Remarkable First Novel," Pasadena (Calif.)
      Star News (18 November), Sec. 1, p. 23.
           Styron's "insights into character and his craftsmanship
      are highly masterful."

120   ZIEGNER, EDWARD. "Here's a First, Not a Last, We Hope," In-
      dianapolis News (8 September), p. 2.
           Lie Down in Darkness "is a book which does not tire you,
      which moves you and which makes you think that here is a
      part of the lives of all of us, bound up in the story of
      this Virginia family."

1952 A BOOKS - NONE

1952 B SHORTER WRITINGS

  1   ANON. "'Writing Can't Be Taught'--Professor, Novelist Talk
      About Success," Charlotte Observer (27 January), p. 15-C.
           Account of Styron's return to speak to a creative writing
      class at Duke University taught by his former teacher, Dr.
      William Blackburn.

  2   ANON. "Human Frailties," London Times (22 March), p. 8.
           In Lie Down in Darkness, Styron's "phrasing, construc-
      tion, method of introducing subsidiary characters, even the
      drive to the funeral which links successive chapters, are
      all reminiscent of Mr. Faulkner, but in a young writer of
      talent such half-conscious imitation is creditable and
      rather endearing."

  3   ANON. "Depressed Areas," Times Literary Supplement (London)
      (28 March), p. 217.
           In Lie Down in Darkness, Styron's "most considerable
      achievement, indeed, is the portrait of the drunken and
      unstable Peyton, who against all odds emerges as a likeable
      and even charming person."

  4   ANON. "Tensions and Adjustments," The Scotsman (Edinburgh)
      (3 April), p. 9.
           Lie Down in Darkness "is a deeply moving and often har-
      rowing work. The imagination displayed in its detail and
      conception alike are of an unusual order."

  5   BLOOMFIELD, PAUL. "New Novels," Manchester (England) Guardian
      (21 March), p. 4.
           Lie Down in Darkness is "pretty sickening stuff."
      Peyton "would have been a perfectly suitable 'heroine' if

the author had been able to assume the right attitude of
detachment instead of flinging himself and trying also to
drag us into the whirlpool."

6   BRIÈRRE, ANNIE. "William Styron," <u>Les Nouvelles Littéraires</u>,
    No. 1302 (14 August), 4.
        Interview in which Sytron discusses <u>Lie Down in Darkness</u>
    and his works-in-progress.

7   BURDICK, RICHARD. "A Remarkable First Novel Treats Group of
    Fascinating People With Great Insight," Sacramento <u>Bee</u> (14
    June), p. 27.
        "Keep your eyes on William Styron; on the basis of this
    first novel the dwindling ranks of major novelists have a
    new member."

8   CHANG, DIANA. "The Emotionally Mature Jew," <u>Congress Weekly</u>,
    19 (18 February), 15-16.
        <u>Lie Down in Darkness</u> "is in some ways an elegy about the
    irretrievability of small moments of life that could have
    made all the difference had the compulsions of personality
    been held in check."

9   FANE, VERNON. "The World of Books," <u>The Sphere</u>, 209 (12
    April), 76.
        <u>Lie Down in Darkness</u> is "all very depressing."

10 H., A. B. Review of <u>Lie Down in Darkness</u>, <u>Punch</u>, 222 (30
    April), 550.
        "The writing, a rare and satisfying mixture of graphic
    realism and subtle impressionism, reaches a very high stan-
    dard, and the story loses none of its effectiveness by
    starting with the dénouement and back-pedalling through
    numerous day-dreams and recollections. Warmly recommended."

11 HAZARD, ELOISE PERRY. "Eight Fiction Finds," <u>Saturday Review
    of Literature</u>, 35 (16 February), 16-18 [17].
        Discussion of Styron's plans, interests, and lifestyle.

12 JANEWAY, ELIZABETH. "Private Emotions Privately Felt," <u>New
    Leader</u>, 35 (21 January), 25.
        In <u>Lie Down in Darkness</u>, Styron effortlessly achieves
    "something that most writers find extremely difficult and
    too many ignore. That is, to plumb private emotion as it
    is felt privately in obscure half-articulate symbols and to
    communicate the weight of this emotion to the reader."

1952

13   JOHNSON, PAMELA HANSFORD. "Father Was Eccentric," John
     O'London's Weekly, 61 (9 May), 464.
          In Lie Down in Darkness, Styron "has the kind of cre-
     ative energy that should eventually find a worthy outlet,
     and I believe it will, when the author is able to free him-
     self of his disastrous self-consciousness."

14   KIRBY, JOHN PENDY. Review of Lie Down in Darkness, Virginia
     Quarterly Review, 28 (Winter), 129-30.
          Although Styron's craftsmanship is "astonishingly ma-
     ture," one would like to see "less reliance on too fre-
     quently resumed literary motifs."

15   LAMBERT, J. W. "New Novels--Every Man in His Humour," London
     Sunday Times (30 March), p. 3.
          In Lie Down in Darkness, "the frontier between true vi-
     tality and facility is ill-defined and perilous, Mr. Styron
     dangerously apt to slip across it."

16   LERMAN, LEO. "Something to Talk About--Bulletin," Mademoiselle,
     34 (January), 112-13, 154 [112, 154].
          Picture of Styron, mention of Lie Down in Darkness, and
     quoted comments from Styron about his future writing plans,
     which "include the writing of a historical novel (probably
     about Nat Turner, the Virginia slave who led a rebellion)."

17   S., A. Review of Lie Down in Darkness, Canadian Forum, 31
     (January), 239.
          "Considered purely on its own merits it stands up well
     by comparison with much modern American fiction; considered
     as a first novel, which it is, it seemed to this reviewer
     to be only slightly short of stupendous."

18   SCOTT, J. D. "New Novels," New Statesman and Nation, 43 (19
     April), 472-73.
          "One's first impression [of Lie Down in Darkness] is of
     something very good indeed; and perhaps it is a little un-
     gracious to note how little there is that is original about
     Mr. Styron's performance."

19   SMITH, HARRISON. "Prose of Promise," Saturday Review of Lit-
     erature, 35 (16 February), 15-16, 42-43 [15].
          Paragraph on Lie Down in Darkness in review of the fic-
     tion of 1951: "Mr. Styron spares his reader nothing in his
     long recital, but he also leaves no doubt that he is to be
     reckoned with in the future."

20   THICKENS, JEAN WILEY. "Book Review--'Lie Down in Darkness'
      Not Pleasant But It's Interesting," Appleton (Wis.) Post-
      Crescent (10 April), p. 14.
           Lie Down in Darkness is "well written and dramatically
      presented but it is not the type of entertainment for the
      tired business man."

21   YAFFE, JAMES. Review of Lie Down in Darkness, Yale Review,
      41 (Winter), viii.
           Basically descriptive review.

1953 A BOOKS - NONE

1953 B SHORTER WRITINGS

1   ANON. "Books--Advance-Guard Advance," Newsweek, 41 (30 March),
     94, 97-98 [94].
          Mention of Styron's contributions to the innaugural is-
     sue of Paris Review and to the new periodical Discovery.

2   BARO, GENE. "A Sampling of New Writers," New York Herald
     Tribune Book Review (8 February), p. 12.
          Review of the first issue of Discovery which includes
     brief favorable mention of Styron's "The Long March."

3   COWLEY, MALCOLM. "American Novels Since the War," New Repub-
     lic, 129 (28 December), 16-18.
          Lie Down in Darkness, along with The Man With the Golden
     Arm, Invisible Man, and The Adventures of Augie March, are
     representative of the most hopeful tendency to be found in
     American fiction in that characters are not presented as
     divorced from society.

4   GEISMAR, MAXWELL. "The End of Something," The Nation, 176
     (14 March), 230-31 [230].
          Review of Discovery with praise for Styron and "The Long
     March": "He is an original--a natural--a writer who makes
     us enjoy the art of writing again."

5   _____. "The Post-War Generation in Arts and Letters," Satur-
     day Review of Literature, 36 (14 March), 11-12, 60.
          Mention that Sytron's prose style has been influenced
     by Wolfe quite as much as by Faulkner.

6   HOLLEY, FRED S. "New Periodical--Styron's Story Dominates,"
     Norfolk Virginian-Pilot (8 February), Part 2, p. 10.

21

1953

        Review of <u>Discovery</u> which praises "The Long March" for
clothing a simple plot with "universal symbols."

7   PARKE, MARY EUGENIA. "Facts & Fiction--Styron Story Featured
       in Original Anthology," Norfolk <u>Virginian-Pilot</u> (4 Januuary),
       Part 5, p. 7.
          Description of "The Long March," which is about to ap-
pear in <u>Discovery</u>.

8   _____. "Facts & Fiction--Promising Americans in France,"
       Norfolk <u>Virginian-Pilot</u> (12 April), Part 2, p. 13.
          Description of first issue of <u>Paris Review</u> and of Styron's
contribution to it.

1954 A BOOKS - NONE

1954 B SHORTER WRITINGS

1   BAKER, MARY JANE, et al. "We Hitch Our Wagons," <u>Mademoiselle</u>,
       39 (August), 266-69 [268].
          Styron is interviewed on novel-writing.

2   DAVIS, ROBERT GORHAM. "In a Ravelled World Love Endures,"
       <u>New York Times Book Review</u> (26 December), pp. 1, 13.
          Styron is mentioned in a group of novelists who still
       write in the fictional modes of the Thirties as opposed to
       the New Novelists. In theme, however, both groups are
       similar.

3   MATTHIESSEN, PETER, and GEORGE PLIMPTON. "William Styron,"
       <u>Paris Review</u>, 2 (Spring), 42-57.
          Interview in which Styron discusses his start as a writ-
       er, his writing habits, the Southern tradition in American
       literature, literary influences on his work, and the liter-
       ary climate in America.
       Reprinted: 1958.B3; 1961.B17.

4   PARKE, MARY EUGENIA. "Facts & Fiction--The Authors Face Crit-
       ics In New York," Norfolk <u>Virginian-Pilot</u> (31 January),
       Part 6, p. 7.
          Brief mention of Styron, who has returned to the United
       States from France and is working on his second novel.

1955 A BOOKS - NONE

1955 B SHORTER WRITINGS

1   ANON. "Countries of the English-Speaking World: News From
     the United States," Times Literary Supplement (London)
     (5 August), pp. II-III.
          Styron and Lie Down in Darkness mentioned briefly.

1956 A BOOKS - NONE

1956 B SHORTER WRITINGS

1   ALDRIDGE, JOHN W. "The Society of Three Novels," in his In
     Search of Heresy. New York: McGraw-Hill, pp. 126-48.
          Styron in Lie Down in Darkness is seen as a Southern
     writer "able to respond to and project back into language
     those intricate relationships between fictional setting and
     human agony."

1957 A BOOKS - NONE

1957 B SHORTER WRITINGS

1   FRIEDMAN, JOSEPH J. "Non-Conformity and the Writer," Venture,
     2 (Winter), 23-31 [27, 29].
          Brief discussion of Peyton in Lie Down in Darkness in
     an article on the modern writer's search for heroes.

1958 A BOOKS - NONE

1958 B SHORTER WRITINGS

1   GEISMAR, MAXWELL. "William Styron: The End of Innocence,"
     in his American Moderns: From Rebellion to Conformity.
     New York: Hill and Wang, pp. 239-50.
          Lie Down in Darkness and "The Long March" are praised
     for evoking "that childhood world of 'illusion' where all
     our feelings were direct and open and full and complete."

2   LICHTENSTEIN, G. "The Exiles," New Statesman and Nation, 55
     (6 September), 320.
          Styron's association with the Paris Review is noted and
     he is seen as one of the modern literary exiles--not in
     rebellion, but part of the literary status quo.

1958

3 MATTHIESSEN, PETER, and GEORGE PLIMPTON. "William Styron,"
    in Writers at Work: The "Paris Review" Interviews. Edited
    by Malcolm Cowley. New York: Viking Press, pp. 268-82.
    Reprint of 1954.B3.

4 STEVENSON, DAVID L. "Fiction's Unfamiliar Face," The Nation,
    187 (1 November), 307-309.
        In an article on the differences between the convention-
    al pre-1945 American novel and the experimental post-1945
    novel, Lie Down in Darkness is cited as a novel in which
    the concept of denouement is irrelevant.

5 TYLER, BETTY. "Bill Styron Works on New Novel In Roxbury
    Isolation," Bridgeport (Conn.) Sunday Post (18 May), p.
    B-3. This article also appeared in Richmond (Va.) Times-
    Dispatch (25 May), pp. 1-L, 4-L.
        Article-interview in which Sytron comments on his novel-
    in-progress (Set This House on Fire) and on his working
    habits.

1959 A BOOKS - NONE

1959 B SHORTER WRITINGS

1 BARR, DONALD. "Lively and Unprecious," New York Times Book
    Review (1 November), p. 40.
        Review of Best Short Stories From "The Paris Review"
    which makes brief mention of Styron's Introduction.

2 BROOKS, RAE. Review of Best Short Stories From "The Paris
    Review," Harper's, 219 (November), 116-18.
        Brief mention of Styron's Introduction.

3 GENTRY, CURT. "A Bookman's Notebook--Stories That Disprove a
    Critical Fiction," San Francisco Chronicle (8 December),
    p. 41.
        Review of Best Short Stories From "The Paris Review"
    which quotes at length and with great praise from Styron's
    Introduction.

4 HODGES, BETTY. "Betty Hodges' Book Nook," Durham (N.C.) Her-
    ald (19 April), p. 5D.
        Includes Styron's comments on Set This House on Fire
    and on reading his works in public.

5 HOOKER, PAT. "Paris Review's Short Stories," Roanoke Times
    (25 October), p. B12.

Review of Best Short Stories From "The Paris Review"
which calls Styron's Introduction "superior to some of the
stories in the anthology."

6   KAZIN, ALFRED. "The Alone Generation," Harper's, 219 (Octo-
     ber), 127-31.
          Styron and Flannery O'Connor are cited as Southern writ-
     ers who are exceptions because they can find the present
     meaningful because they find the past so.
     Reprinted: 1962.B22.

7   MENN, THORPE. "Books of the Day," Kansas City Star (4 July),
     p. 16.
          Brief mention of and quotes from Styron's Introduction
     in pre-publication review of Best Short Stories From "The
     Paris Review."

8   O'ROURKE, ELIZABETH. Review of Best Short Stories From "The
     Paris Review," Best Sellers, 19 (1 November), 259.
          Brief laudatory mention of Styron's Introduction.

1960 A BOOKS - NONE

1960 B SHORTER WRITINGS

1   ADAMS, PHOEBE. Review of Set This House on Fire, Atlantic
     Monthly, 206 (July), 97-98.
          "Mr. Styron is one of those novelists who assume that
     serious purpose constitutes a license to bore."

2   ALDINGER, BEATRICE I. Review of Set This House on Fire,
     Charleston (S.C.) News & Courier (5 June), Sec. C, p. 13.
          It is a "lusty book that jolts the reader with its con-
     cepts of the varieties of good and evil--mostly evil."

3   ALEXANDER, CHARLES. "Comes Now Styron With His Second Novel
     of Moderns," Albany (Ore.) Democrat-Herald (30 July), p.
     10.
          Basically descriptive favorable review of Set This House
     on Fire.

4   ANON. "The Housatonic," Horizon, 2 (May), 10-29 [28].
          Styron briefly profiled among a number of creative peo-
     ple who live in Housatonic River area of Connecticut.

5   ANON. "Lucidity Could Do Wonders," Charlotte News (4 June),
     p. 7B.

1960

> Although Set This House on Fire shows that Styron "is not without fine talent and many readers will doubtless find great meaning in his efforts," the reviewer prefers "writing of precision, lucidity and structural strength."

6   ANON. "Arty People Flounder In Own Morass," St. Louis Globe Democrat (5 June), p. 4F
        "If we are to judge by the Styron stripe" in Set This House on Fire, "the world's in such a mess it isn't worth saving...."

7   ANON. "Empty Soul Blues," Time, 74 (6 June), 98.
        Set This House on Fire is a "507 page crying jag."

8   ANON. "Just Out: A Kind of Tenderness," Newsweek, 55 (6 June), 117-18.
        In Set This House on Fire, Styron "creates the singular sense that his blood stream is somehow in circulation with the rest of the human race and that the pain upon which he broods is not exclusively his own."

9   ANON. "Life, Death of Sadistic Millionaire," Miami Herald (12 June), p. 14-J.
        "It would seem that we have had enough of beatniks and psychopaths but [in Set This House on Fire] the author of Lie Down in Darkness gives a new slant on this new, dark world."

10 ANON. Review of Set This House on Fire, Virginia Quarterly Review, 36 (Autumn), civ, cvi.
        "It is frightening to see so much talent wasted on such tawdry material."

11 ANON. Review of Set This House on Fire, New Mexico Quarterly, 30 (Winter), 412.
        It is a "worthy successor to Styron's first novel...."

12 BARLEY, REX. "Styron's Second Novel Falls Short of First," Los Angeles Mirror News (20 June), Part II, p. 2.
        Because the characters in Set This House on Fire "never quite live up to their promise," little of the novel "will linger in the memory. Styron can, and will, do better than this."

13 BARO, GENE. "Styron's New Novel: Search For the Meaning of Evil," New York Herald Tribune Book Review (5 June), pp. 1, 12.

> In Set This House on Fire, "one regrets the failures the more because there is so much merit here, so much to interest one seriously."

14   BETTS, DORIS. "Serious Violent Novel," Houston Post (12 June), Houston Now Section, p. 36.
     Set This House on Fire combines "a novel of serious intent with a can't-put-it-down plot of action" and is "the best thing this reviewer has read in many years."

15   BORKLUND, ELMER. "Fiction of Violence and Pain," Commentary, 30 (November), 452-54.
     Set This House on Fire is "undermined by the shallowness of Styron's attacks on American life" which are "primitive and superficial."

16   BOROFF, DAVID. "The Styron Novel," New York Post (5 June), Magazine, p. 11.
     Set This House on Fire is "not only an enthralling novel but an arduous reaching out towards values at a time when emptiness is an intellectual vogue."

17   BOURG, GENE. "Italy Is Scene of American Drama," New Orleans Times-Picayune (19 June), Sec. 2, p. 3.
     Set This House on Fire is "one of the most provocative pieces of fiction to come to this reader's attention in a long time."

18   BRADLEY, VAN ALLEN. "Bradley on Books--Second Styron Novel Close to a Masterpiece," Chicago Daily News (4 June), p. 13.
     In Set This House on Fire, Styron "writes like an angel, with Faulknerian overtones and occasional echoes of Hawthorne and Poe."

19   BREIT, HARVEY. "A Second Novel," Partisan Review, 27 (Summer), 561-63.
     "For me, who may be only a poor minority, Set This House on Fire is an immeasurable gain in maturity over the author's fine first novel...."

20   BRUNI, THOMAS G. Review of Set This House on Fire, Lehigh Valley (Penna.) Labor Herald (29 June), p. 5.
     Set This House on Fire is "overlong, overlush and overdone."

21   [BURTON, HAL]. "A Novel of Rare Quality," Newsday (Garden City, N.Y.) (4 June), p. 31.

1960

"As a story of agony and redemption," Set This House on Fire "is one of the fine novels of our time."

22 CHAFFEE, NORMAN. "Examination of Good, Evil," Tulsa Sunday World (10 July), Your World Magazine, p. 17.
    In Set This House on Fire, Styron "still has the ability to do things with words in the same way an artist uses a paint brush but the magic of the first novel is not fully reflected in the second."

23 CHENEY, FRANCES NEEL. "Rich, Sensitive Prose; Eye for Detail," Nashville Banner (3 June), p. 24.
    Set This House on Fire is too long and needs "a bit more restraint in some of the frank descriptions."

24 COVICI, PASCAL, JR. "Powerful Vision For Our Time," Dallas Morning News (5 June), Sec. 5, p. 6.
    In Set This House on Fire, "the artistry with which Styron presents the struggles of his people to come to grips with themselves is as stirring as the breadth of incident."

25 CREED, HOWARD. "Styron Doesn't Set Reviewer on Fire," Birmingham (Ala.) News (21 August), p. 8-E.
    "I suspect a good many readers will find" Set This House on Fire "confusing or boring or maybe both."

26 CULLIGAN, GLENDY. "Styron Returns--Jury Still Hung," Washington Post (5 June), p. 6-E.
    "The best verdict that a literary jury can return, after weighing this massive testimony to Styron's genius [Set This House on Fire], is still the inconclusive 'Not proven.'"

27 CUNNINGHAM, BILL. "Styron Novel Is Intricate," San Antonio Express and News (10 July), p. 5-G.
    In Set This House on Fire, even though Styron "drags his characters to the depths," the novel "retains a magic of writing that lures the reader on and on, perhaps hoping for a sudden change in the two men."

28 CURLEY, THOMAS F. "The Quarrel With Time in American Fiction," American Scholar, 29 (Autumn), 552-60 [558-60].
    "To be brief, Set This House on Fire is not the kind of book I expected from Styron; maybe I should say it's not the kind of book I wanted; but of its kind, it is very good, especially in the detail and thoroughness of characterization."

28

29 DAHMS, JOSEPH G. Review of Set This House on Fire, America,
103 (18 June), 380-81.
"The book as a whole is not better than the sum of its
parts."

30 DANIELS, N. A. "The Identity of Opposites," San Francisco
People's World (9 July), p. 6.
In Set This House on Fire, "it is almost impossible to
feel anything for his [Styron's] hyperesthetic artist; less
for his psychopath."

31 DAVIS, ROBERT GORHAM. "Styron and the Students," Critique
(Minneapolis), 3 (Summer), 37-46.
The language of Set This House on Fire is explored with
a writing class and a growing dissatisfaction with Styron
is expressed.

32 DAWKINS, CECIL. "Our Man In Italy--A Study of Evil and Its
Expiation," Milwaukee Journal (5 June), Sec. 5, p. 4.
In Set This House on Fire, "faults diminish but do not
destroy the novel's power."

33 DIDION, JOAN. "Fiction Chronicle--Inadequate Mirrors," National Review, 8 (2 July), 430-31.
Although Set This House on Fire is "about twice as long
as it should be" and "even cut in half,...it would be no-
where near as good as" Lie Down in Darkness, Styron "is
still running far ahead of the pack."

34 DWIGHT, OGDEN G. "In 'Set This House on Fire' Styron Has
Quite a Blaze," Des Moines Register (3 July), p. 11-G.
Set This House on Fire "explores latter-day human val-
ues, motives and morals searchingly."

35 EVANS, DERRO. "Fiction Gains New Stature With William Styron
Novel," Amarillo (Texas) Sunday News-Globe (5 June), p. 6-C.
Set This House on Fire "is good; it is superior; it is
excellent. Time alone will tell whether it is great."

36 FENTON, CHARLES A. "William Styron and the Age of the Slob,"
South Atlantic Quarterly, 59 (Autumn), 469-76.
In Set This House on Fire, "what Styron has undertaken,
and what he has in large part achieved, is nothing less
than a rendition of national mood dramatized in terms of
powerful characters of fiction."

37 FERGUSON, ANNA LAWRENCE. "Bits About Books--New Styron Novel,"
Norfolk Virginian-Pilot and Portsmouth Star (1 May), p. 6-F.

1960

   Brief mention of Styron's forthcoming novel, Set This
House on Fire.

38   FOSTER, RICHARD. "An Orgy of Commerce: William Styron's Set
      This House on Fire," Critique (Minneapolis), 3 (Summer),
      59-70.
         Styron is much overrated and Set This House on Fire is
      a simple story "stretched, stuffed and padded" to give it
      the apparent scope and poundage of a "great" mind.

39   FRENCH, MARION FLOOD. "Maine Bookmarks," Bangor Daily News
      (18-19 June), p. 7.
         Set This House on Fire "still proclaims this young man's
      command of the thunder and lightening of literary skill....
      But what this young man has to say, in this instance, seems
      to be that his viewpoint is very young."

40   FULLER, EDMUND. "A Picture of Hell By a Writer of Maturing
      Vision," Chicago Sunday Tribune Magazine of Books (5 June),
      p. 3.
         With Set This House on Fire, Styron's "development looms
      larger and more important on our literary horizon."

41   GENTRY, CURT. "Styron's Superb Third Novel," San Francisco
      Sunday Chronicle (5 June), This World Magazine, p. 22.
         Set This House on Fire "may be one of the finest novels
      of our times."

42   GOSSMAN, OTIS. "Bits About Books--Raising a Writer," Norfolk
      Virginian-Pilot and Portsmouth Star (29 May), p. 14-A.
         Interview with Styron's father who speaks of his son's
      fiction and of how he raised him.

43   GRIFFIN, LLOYD W. Review of Set This House on Fire, Library
      Journal, 85 (15 June), 2458.
         It is "an excellent novel, highly recommended, but not
      for the squeamish."

44   HALL, BARBARA HODGE. "New Novel By Styron Is Gripping,"
      Anniston (Ala.) Star (10 July), p. 6B.
         Set This House on Fire fulfills Styron's "past promise,
      for it is highly readable and masterfully constructed."

45   HAYES, E. NELSON. "Novels By Styron and Fifield," Providence
      Sunday Journal (5 June), p. 20-W.
         Set This House on Fire "exemplifies two of the major
      faults which characterize much American fiction, faults

involving the realization of tragedy, and the voice of the
novelist."

46   HICKS, GRANVILLE. "After the Fury, a Time of Peace," Saturday
      Review of Literature, 43 (4 June), 13.
            "A novel as rich and deep, as carefully wrought as [Set
      This House on Fire] takes more thinking about than a re-
      viewer with a deadline can give it."

47   HIGHET, GILBERT. Review of Set This House on Fire, Book-of-
      the-Month Club News (May), p. 7.
            It is "a tribute to Mr. Styron's skill with his language
      and his gift for manipulating people that he carries you
      on, over waves of nausea, to the last word of his long and
      complex novel."

48   HODGES, BETTY. "Betty Hodges' Book Nook," Durham (N.C.) Morn-
      ing Herald (24 January), p. 5D.
            Advance blurb for Set This House on Fire which gives a
      plot summary and reprints publisher's praise for the book.

49   _____. "Betty Hodges' Book Nook," Durham (N.C.) Morning Her-
      ald (3 July), p. 5D.
            Largely descriptive favorable review of Set This House
      on Fire.

50   HOEY, REID A. "Styron's New Novel of Good and Evil," Baltimore
      Sunday Sun (6 June), Sec. A, p. 5.
            "We would not presume to advise William Styron on his
      future; he knows where he is going, and he is going far.
      In fact he may have already arrived. But does he need to
      depress us so much? Upset us so greatly? Make us think
      so deeply?"

51   HOLLANDER, JOHN. Review of Set This House on Fire, Yale Re-
      view, 50 (Fall), 152-53.
            It is a book of "well-handled moments," but neither nar-
      rator "manages to escape a kind of Humanities-lecturing
      tone that comes, too directly, from the author's own para-
      digms of the book's tragic movement."

52   HUMMEL, JOSEPH W. "'Set This House on Fire'--Novel Stresses
      Finding Identity," Columbia Missourian (12 June), Sec. B,
      p. 7.
            If Lie Down in Darkness "is better for being shorter,"
      Set This House on Fire "is outstanding for its integration
      of what could have been unnecessary detail."

1960

53   HUNTER, ANNA C.   "Styron Fulfills Promise With Explosive New
      Novel," Savannah <u>Morning News</u> (5 June), Magazine, p. 14.
          <u>Set This House on Fire</u> is a "novel of heroic proportions
      not set on Olympic heights, but in the squalor of degraded
      labyrinths of experience."

54   HUTCHENS, JOHN K.   Review of <u>Set This House on Fire</u>, New York
      <u>Herald Tribune</u> (3 June), p. 11.
          "The best of <u>Set This House on Fire</u> is brilliant. Over-
      shadowing it, and virtually drowning it, is all that is
      overdone and unnecessary."

55   HUTCHISON, RUTH.   "Reviewer's Corner--Styron's New Book May
      Raise Alarms," Bethlehem (Penna.) <u>Globe-Times</u> (11 June),
      Sec. 3, p. 19.
          <u>Set This House on Fire</u> is "a soiled F. Scott Fitzgerald
      combined with a snarling William Faulkner, reminiscent of
      both but lacking their touch of genius."

56   JOHNSON, C. W.   "Finding New Pieces in Old Tale," Springfield
      (Mo.) <u>Sunday News & Leader</u> (5 June), p. B5.
          Largely descriptive review of <u>Set This House on Fire</u>.

57   J[ONES], C[ARTER] B[ROOKE].   "Mr. Styron's New Novel Is a Dis-
      appointment," Washington (D.C.) <u>Sunday Star</u> (5 June), p.
      11-C.
          <u>Set This House on Fire</u> is, "despite its obvious merits,
      disappointing."

58   KAUFMAN, CLARENCE.   "Second Styron Novel Proof of Major Tal-
      ent," Lincoln (Neb.) <u>Sunday Journal and Star</u> (5 June), p.
      12-B.
          <u>Set This House on Fire</u> is "not the year's best novel,
      but it reveals many others as the inferior efforts they
      are."

59   KENNEY, HERBERT, JR.   "Moralizing Binge Spoils Styron Talent,"
      Indianapolis <u>News</u> (6 August), p. 2.
          In <u>Set This House on Fire</u>, "good and evil battle it out
      for 507 pages, with a decision that will surprise no one."

60   KIRSCH, ROBERT R.   "Books and People--Styron's 'House' Nears
      Greatness," Los Angeles <u>Times</u> (5 June), Sec. C, p. 7.
          <u>Set This House on Fire</u> is "one of the finest novels I
      have read in a decade."

61   KOHLER, DAYTON.   "Virginia Author: Styron Treats Moral Issues
      Dramatically," Richmond (Va.) <u>News Leader</u> (8 June), p. 13.

Set This House on Fire is "a considerable advance over"
Lie Down in Darkness; it "presents unsparingly but compas-
sionately the causes and configuration of man's guilt, the
struggle of innocence and self to survive in the fragmented
life of our time."

62   KOHN, SHERWOOD. "The Book Scene--Styron...an Heir of Camus?"
     Louisville Times (15 June), p. 11.
         Set This House on Fire is a "provocative, economical,
     lucid piece of writing, completely consistent with itself,
     neatly and comprehensively plotted in depth."

63   KRIEGER, ROBERT E. "Unending Nightmare of Good Versus Evil,"
     Worcester Sunday Telegram (5 June), Sec. E, p. 9.
         "Just reading [Set This House on Fire] brings back a hope
     that perhaps the day of the carefully planned, plotted and
     absorbing novel has not gone."

64   L., E. H. "New Book Plenty Hot--It Deserves to Burn," Salt
     Lake City Tribune (14 August), p. 15-W.
         Set This House on Fire is "so vile, so revolting that it
     cannot be ignored."

65   L., T. C. "New Book Suffers From Overwriting," Columbia (S.C.)
     Record (17 November), p. 4-D.
         "Those with plenty of reading time will enjoy this trav-
     elogue [Set This House on Fire], but most readers would
     prefer a condensed version."

66   LAWSON, JOHN HOWARD. "William Styron: Darkness and Fire in
     the Modern Novel," Mainstream, 13 (October), 9-18.
         Set This House on Fire, "so brilliant and yet so murky,
     so shadowed with darkness and consumed with fire," is an
     intensified example of concepts and tendencies presented in
     the books of other writers.

67   L[AYCOCK], E[DWARD] A. "American Spoiled Boy--Styron's Third
     Novel Shocking, Powerful Picture of Degradation," Boston
     Sunday Globe (5 June), p. 7-A.
         Set This House on Fire "has the impact of the thrust of
     an outer space satellite."

68   LAYTON, MIKE. "Critics' Predictions Fulfilled by Styron,"
     Olympia (Wash.) Sunday Olympian (12 June), p. 22.
         In Set This House on Fire, Styron "explores the awaken-
     ing of a man, the conflict of lurking evil with indifferent
     goodness and brings out of it a story that puts to shame

1960

all others of American expatriates, from Henry James to
Papa Hemingway."

69   LEA, GEORGE. "New Novel Won't Set House on Fire," Chicago
       Sun-Times (10 July), Sec. 3, p. 5.
           In Set This House on Fire, "what Styron is so very seri-
       ous about is impotence. His concern would not seem to be
       baseless."

70   LINDAU, BETSY. Review of Set This House on Fire, Asheville
       (N.C.) Citizen-Times (5 June), p. 3-D.
           Set This House on Fire "makes clear the reason Styron's
       name is mentioned in company with the most distinguished
       novelists of the day."

71   LITTLEWOOD, SANDRA. "Bad, Good Are Mixed In Styron," Sacra-
       mento Bee (5 June), p. L30.
           Although Styron "has a wonderful gift for characteriza-
       tion, narrative, dialog and description," the reader of
       Set This House on Fire "cannot help hoping that the next
       time [he] sits down to write a novel he equips himself with
       a box of blue pencils as well as a typewriter."

72   LOWMAN, ANN. "Too Much Retrospect Mars Styron's Second,"
       Columbus (Ohio) Sunday Dispatch (26 June), TAB Section, p.
       12.
           In Set This House on Fire, "the writer has let his per-
       sonality analyses get away from him. And the book suffers."

73   McDERMOTT, STEPHANIE. "Arty People Flounder in Own Morass,"
       St. Louis Globe Democrat (5 June), p. 4-F.
           Styron makes "a good story" out of Set This House on
       Fire, and "he can make his characters come alive. But af-
       ter wading through 500 pages of it, one wishes he hadn't
       created them at all."

74   McMANIS, JOHN. "Such Fascinating Villains," Detroit News (5
       June), p. 3-F.
           In Set This House on Fire, Styron "shows a fine selec-
       tion of material and a wit that is scathing, devastating,
       tart, and sardonic."

75   MAILER, NORMAN. Advertisements For Myself. New York: New
       American Library, pp. 415-16.
           Styron will be the most important writer of his genera-
       tion.

76   MALCOLM, DONALD. "False Alarm," New Yorker, 36 (4 June), 152-
        54.
              In Set This House on Fire, Styron "manages the unusual
        feat of stimulating the reader's curiosity without ever
        arousing his interest."

77   MALIN, IRVING. "Styron Probes Ancient Truths In New Novel,"
        Fort Wayne News-Sentinel (4 June), p. 4.
              Set This House on Fire "is one of the most powerful Amer-
        erican novels of the last 20 years."

78   MASON, ROBERT. "Characters Clash In Heroic Conflict," Norfolk
        Virginian-Pilot and Portsmouth Star (5 June), p. 8-F.
              In Set This House on Fire, Styron "has lost none of his
        writing talent," but "he has confused...pornography with
        philosophy."

79   MAY, WILLIAM. "A Disappointment," Newark (N.J.) Sunday News
        (12 June), Sec. 2, p. W22.
              Set This House on Fire is an example of "a good writer
        wasting his time....The three men [Styron] writes about are
        so hollow and unappetizing that even the sympathetic reader,
        who goes on to the end hoping Styron will somehow regain
        his balance, winds up feeling depressed."

80   MILLER, NOLAN. Review of Set This House on Fire, Antioch Re-
        view, 20 (Summer), 256.
              "With William Styron one has to say now, 'He must be
        read.' And that means all of him."

81   MIZENER, ARTHUR. "Some People of Our Time," New York Times
        Book Review (5 June), pp. 5, 26.
              In Set This House on Fire, "the trouble is that all of
        this sharply observed and represented material is solemnly
        hopped up, emotionally and metaphysically."

82   MOHRT, MICHEL. "Michel Mohrt présente la première révélation
        du roman Américain depuis la guerre: j'ai vécu avec William
        Styron la dolce vita," Arts, No. 786 (7-13 September), 3.

83   MONAGHAN, CHARLES. "Styronic Manner," Commonweal, 72 (22
        July), 380.
              In Set This House on Fire, Styron's "romantic procliv-
        ities are the undoing of what might have been a brilliant
        work."

84   MOONEY, HARRY, JR. "Styron Raises Issues, Faces Them Squarely,
        But Novel Is Seriously Marred By Author's Undisciplined

1960

Rhetoric," Pittsburgh <u>Press</u> (5 June), Sec. 5, p. 14.
<u>Set This House on Fire</u> is "seriously marred by the un-
fortunate and undisciplined rhetoric on which it relies."

85   MORELAND, JOHN. "Critic on the Hearth...," Oakland (Calif.)
<u>Tribune</u> (15 June), p. D23.
      <u>Set This House on Fire</u> is "ill-constructed; its charac-
ters are hopelessly naif and loutish; it is filled with unnecessary obscenity and scenes which cannot even be described
as debauchery, because they are so dull; and the style is
not so much 'handsome' as it is over-ornamented."

86   MURRAY, JAMES G. Review of <u>Set This House on Fire</u>, <u>The Critic</u>,
19 (August-September), 37.
      "The reader is involved but not enlightened (in fact,
not even extricated) even as the writer seems to be furi-
ously engaged but never clearly and absolutely committed."

87   NEWBERRY, MIKE. "Shock of Recognition," <u>Mainstream</u>, 13 (September), 61-63.
      In <u>Set This House on Fire</u>, how "can the conflict be a
true one, dramatically and morally, if all the characters
are drawn from the same milieu, have similar philosophies,
and bespeak the same degradation?"

88   NICHOLS, LEWIS. "Background," <u>New York Times Book Review</u> (5
June), p. 8.
      Notes on Styron's writing of <u>Set This House on Fire</u>, in-
cluding autobiographical elements in the novel.

89   NICHOLS, LUTHER. "Styron's Literary Shock Treatment," San
Francisco <u>Examiner</u> (29 May), Highlight Section, p. 6.
      <u>Set This House on Fire</u> "should rank among the major
achievements of American writers in the 20th century."

90   NORMAN, SUE. "Styron Survives Second Novel Test In Style,"
San Angelo (Texas) <u>Standard Times</u> (11 September), Sec. B,
p. 8.
      <u>Set This House on Fire</u> is "an unforgettable book."

91   O'LEARY, THEODORE M. "All the Elements of Greatness," Kansas
City <u>Star</u> (4 June), p. 18.
      In <u>Set This House on Fire</u>, "like great music, Styron's
prose is often highly charged with emotion, often exudes
a sensuous quality."

92   PECKHAM, STANTON. "Styron's Second Novel Fulfills Promise,"
Denver <u>Sunday Post</u> (5 June), <u>Roundup</u> Section, p. 9.

Set This House on Fire is "a powerful novel, as powerful
in its way as the wartime novels to which it seems the nat-
ural successor--and likewise as surrealistic."

93 PERKIN, ROBERT L. "Important Fiction," Rocky Mountain News
    (Denver) (26 June), p. 14-A.
        Set This House on Fire is "important contemporary fic-
    tion; the naturalism is neither titillating nor self-ser-
    ving."

94 PICKREL, PAUL. "Heroic Proportions," Harper's, 221 (July),
    93.
        Set This House on Fire is "an impressive book"; Styron's
    "great resource is excess."

95 PRESCOTT, ORVILLE. "Books of The Times," New York Times (3
    June), p. 29.
        Set This House on Fire is a "hollow and windy book that
    fails to live up to its own highfalutin mannas (quotations
    from Donne, meaningless tirades on art, sex, the times and
    seasons)."

96 PRICE, EMERSON. "Magnificent Novel Portrays Man Trapped By
    His Own Folly," Cleveland Press (7 June), p. 28.
        Set This House on Fire is "one of the most astonishing
    pieces of creative writing to appear--either in America or
    elsewhere--in a very long time."

97 RAGAN, MARJORIE. "A Brilliant Fire of Tragedy," Raleigh News
    and Observer (5 June), Sec. 3, p. 5.
        Set This House on Fire demonstrates that "Mr. Styron can
    really write. He can really involve you with the lives of
    his characters."

98 RAGAN, SAM. "Southern Accent," Raleigh News and Observer (19
    June), Sec. 3, p. 5.
        A letter from Styron's father is quoted, providing brief
    biographical details about William Styron and expressing
    the elder Styron's pleasure over the publication of Set This
    House on Fire.

99 RICHMAN, CHARLES. "Books," Brooklyn (N.Y.) Record (17 June),
    p. 6.
        Brief, descriptive and favorable review of Set This House
    on Fire.

100 ROGERS, W. G. "Killing In Italy Theme of New Styron Novel,"
    Cleveland Plain Dealer (12 June), p. 8-H. This syndicated

1960

review also appeared in Santa Barbara (Calif.) <u>News Press</u>
(5 June); Long Beach (Calif.) <u>Independent Press Telegram</u>
(12 June).
<u>Set This House on Fire</u> "over all provides a fine discern-
ment, with a wit that is tart, bawdy or sardonic."

101 ROHM, ZETA. Review of <u>Set This House on Fire</u>, Seattle <u>Post-
Intelligencer</u> (11 June), p. 13.
"Mr. Styron has a wonderful compassion for the many
weirdies, phonies, over-sexed hangers-on he has created,"
but <u>Set This House on Fire</u> is rambling and as "anticlimactic
as Key-Stone cops."

102 ROTHBERG, ABRAHAM. "Styron's Appointment in Sambuco," <u>New
Leader</u>, 43 (4-11 July), 24-27.
<u>Set This House on Fire</u> is "a magnificent book, whose
pages--at least for me--echo with Melville and Faulkner and
Fitzgerald."

103 ROWE, PERCY. "Monster and Madman--Meet the Terrible Twins,"
Toronto <u>Telegram</u> (8 October), p. 59.
With <u>Set This House on Fire</u>, Styron "soars immediately
to the top rung of writers in the sixties."

104 RUBIN, LOUIS D., JR. Review of <u>Set This House on Fire</u>, Baltimore <u>Evening Sun</u> (3 June), p. 30.
If <u>Set This House on Fire</u> "is not a fully realized fiction, it is nonetheless a novel of great parts and tremen-
dously moving and believable people; it displays an artistry
of language and a perception of character almost unique in
Mr. Styron's generation of writers."

105 _____, KATHERINE ANNE PORTER, FLANNERY O'CONNOR, CAROLINE
GORDON, and MADISON JONES. <u>Recent Southern Fiction: A
Panel Discussion</u>. Macon: Wesleyan College, pp. 8-10.
Brief discussion of Styron as a Southern writer centering
on the sense of community in <u>Lie Down in Darkness</u>, and on
Styron's ability to generate genuine feeling.

106 SCHNEIDER, HAROLD W. "Two Bibliographies: Saul Bellow, William
Styron," <u>Critique</u> (Minneapolis), 3 (Summer), 71-91.
Listing of works by and about Styron, with annotations
provided for "the most important" pieces.

107 SHERMAN, JOHN K. "Melodrama of Good and Evil Probes Human
Undercurrents," Minneapolis <u>Tribune</u> (12 June), p. 6-E.
<u>Set This House on Fire</u> is "engrossing reading, although
one feels that it is overwritten and has overshot the mark."

108   SIMMONDS, ANNE. "A Successful Young Writer Hails From the
      Peninsula," Newport News (Va.) Times-Herald (2 June), p.
      17.
           Description of Set This House on Fire, review of Styron's
      career to date, and brief comments by Styron's father on
      his son's writing habits.

109   SINCLAIR, REID B. "From the Fiction Shelf--Prodigious Effort
      By Virginian," Richmond (Va.) Times Dispatch (26 June), p.
      10-L.
           Those who read Set This House on Fire "will be disap-
      pointed by its sensationalism, both in incident and lan-
      guage, and even by its demands on one's credulity."

110   SNYDER, MARY RENNELS. "Behind the Backs of Books & Authors,"
      Gary (Ind.) Post-Tribune (5 June), p. D-9.
           "Be of strong fibre if you read [Set This House on Fire].
      You will be amply repaid for your courage."

111   SOUTHERN, TERRY. Review of Set This House on Fire, The Nation,
      191 (19 November), 382.
           In Set This House on Fire, Styron has written from "a
      literary orientation instead of from a personal one...and
      that would seem to be a fundamental responsibility for a
      writer of his status and opportunity."

112   STEVENSON, DAVID L. "Styron and the Fiction of the Fifties,"
      Critique (Minneapolis), 3 (Summer), 47-58.
           Praise for Lie Down in Darkness; but Set This House on
      Fire is seen as unrealized. Styron and his generation of
      writers have abandoned social man for the unconditioned in
      man.
      Reprinted: 1963.B26.

113   STRATTON, JAMES C. "Footnotes and Fancies--Moral Decay Exam
      Reveals and Revolts," Stillwater (Okla.) News-Press (24
      April), p. 9.
           Set This House on Fire is "continually revealing and al-
      though it is frequently discouraging, one cannot dismiss
      it with a shrug."

114   SULLIVAN, WALTER. "New Styron Disappoints," Nashville Tennes-
      sean (19 June), p. 10-D.
           Set This House on Fire "ought to be more competent tech-
      nically and more profound in concept. Styron is no longer
      a beginning writer now, and in a third novel one can hardly
      be content with mere promise."

1960

115   TAYLOR, ROBERT W. "World of Books," <u>Diplomat,</u> 11 (July), 40.
       In <u>Set This House on Fire</u>, "Styron intends to shock...and
       does, with devastating effect."

116   TYLER, BETTY. "Roxbury Author's Second: Provocative, Disturb-
       ing," Bridgeport (Conn.) <u>Sunday Post</u> (29 May), p. C-4.
       In <u>Set This House on Fire</u>, Styron "has advanced. His
       writing is even better and his approach to life has grown.
       He still is talky, very very talky but this speech is so
       powerful that the reader savors every word and is absorbed
       in the strong imagery."

117   W., J. "Books In Review," Auburn (N.Y.) <u>Citizen-Advertiser</u> (4
       June), p. 4.
       Although Styron, in <u>Set This House on Fire</u>, makes his
       characters believable, "he does not...make us care very much
       what happens to any of them." But the new novel is "a ma-
       jor work" and "worth the wait."

118   WADE, GERALD. "Conflict of Evil and Search for Peace Is Awe-
       somely Told," Beaumont (Texas) <u>Journal</u> (17 June), p. 20.
       <u>Set This House on Fire</u> is "one of the most brilliant and
       more important novels of the year."

119   WATTS, HAROLD H. "Assembly of Horrors," St. Louis <u>Post-Dis-</u>
       <u>patch</u> (19 June), p. 4-B.
       <u>Set This House on Fire</u> is "a book full of moral frenzy
       that leaves nothing more permanent than tidemarks."

120   YARUS, W.P. "<u>Set This House on Fire</u>: Novelist Grows in Stat-
       ure," Charlotte <u>Observer</u> (12 June), p. 7-B.
       <u>Set This House on Fire</u> has "a wealth of material both in
       the narrative and philosophic aspects."

1961 A BOOKS - NONE

1961 B SHORTER WRITINGS

1   ANON. "New Fiction," London <u>Times</u> (16 February), p. 15.
       In <u>Set This House on Fire</u>, "Mr. Styron, by double-dyeing
       both characters and style, does not add force to his impas-
       sioned morality--he merely exhausts our sympathies and blunts
       our sensations, overstraining his considerable imaginative
       talent."

2   ANON. "What Happened at Sambuco," <u>Times Literary Supplement</u>
       (London) (17 February), p. 101.

In Set This House on Fire, there is "no doubt at all
about Mr. Styron's grotesque and luxuriant talent. Perhaps
one day he will find a fully adequate form for expressing
it."

3   ANON. "New Novels: On the Operatic Scale," The Scotsman (Ed-
     inburgh) (25 February), Week-End Magazine, p. 2.
          "There is undoubted power in this colossal work [Set This
     House on Fire], undoubted vigour of style, intensely vivid
     description. But is such a lingering journey through the
     passions really necessary?"

4   ANON. "A Quick Look at the Rest of the Books," London Evening
     Standard (28 February), p. 17.
          Set This House on Fire is "overlong, over-conscious, but
     written with flaring talent."

5   BAUMBACH, JONATHAN. "The Theme of Guilt and Redemption in the
     Post Second World War Novel." Ph.D. dissertation, Stanford
     University, 1961 [Abstracted in Dissertation Abstracts, 22
     (November), 1620-21].
          Chapter on Lie Down in Darkness. Revised version of this
     thesis appears as 1965.B3. See also 1964.B4.

6   BRYDEN, RONALD. "Near Amalfi," The Spectator, No. 6921 (17
     February), 232-33.
          Set This House on Fire "is too crammed with matter to
     succeed wholly, but such rich congestion cannot wholly
     fail."

7   CLEARY, PAL. "New Fiction," Books and Bookmen, 8 (March), 27.
          In Set This House on Fire, Styron's "romantic procliv-
     ities are the undoing of what might have been a brilliant
     work."

8   [COATES, JOHN T.] "The Men Among Us: Profile of a Best-Selling
     Author," New Englander, 35 (November), 18.
          Account of Styron's career to date, with brief autobio-
     graphical comments included.

9   FRIEDMAN, MELVIN J. "William Styron: An Interim Appraisal,"
     English Journal, 50 (March), 149-58, 192.
          Examination of Styron's career to date. Styron is a cen-
     tral figure in contemporary fiction who profits from the
     work of his contemporaries, but demands tighter structure
     for the novel, more concern with style, more completely
     "rounded" characters.
     Reprinted: 1967.A1; 1970.A1; 1974.A2.

1961

10 GEORGE, DANIEL. "Recent Fiction--Bearer of the World's Des-
       pair," London Daily Telegraph and Morning Post (17 February),
       p. 19.
            Set This House on Fire is a "bloated tale of civilised
       horrors" that "refuses to admit the necessity for a breath-
       ing-space."

11 GILLON, DIANA, and MEIR GILLON. "Fiction of the Week--Extra-
       ordinary Vices," London Sunday Times (19 February), Magazine
       Section, p. 27.
            Despite the excellences of Set This House on Fire, "Mr.
       Styron is a good enough writer to deal just as excitingly
       with normal people."

12 HASSAN, IHAB. "Encounter With Necessity: Three Novels By
       Styron, Swados, and Mailer," in his Radical Innocence:
       Studies in the Contemporary American Novel. Princeton,
       N.J.: Princeton University Press, pp. 124-52.
            Focuses on Peyton Loftis in Lie Down in Darkness with
       respect to three realms: social, domestic, and private.
       Concludes that she is a scapegoat figure, both innocent and
       guilty, but without any resolution.
       Reprinted: 1964.B9; 1970.A1.

13 _____. "The Avant-Garde: Which Way Is Forward?" The Nation,
       193 (18 November), 396-99.
            Speculations on the direction of the American novel which
       note especially the lack of social consciousness among
       Styron and others. Set This House on Fire is cited briefly
       as one view of the existential hero.

14 HILL, SUSAN. Review of Set This House on Fire, Time and Tide,
       42 (24 February), 285.
            "It is a book you have to read, because it says, in the
       end, almost all that matters about life."

15 LEWIS, R. W. B. "American Letters: A Projection," Yale Review,
       51 (December), 211-26.
            Styron is among several American writers of the post-war
       generation mentioned.

16 McNAMARA, EUGENE. "William Styron's Long March: Absurdity
       and Authority," Western Humanities Review, 15 (Summer),
       267-72.
            Examination of plot, structure, and especially metaphor
       in The Long March. Concludes that the novel closely re-
       flects "the tenor of our own time."

17   [MATTHIESSEN, PETER, and GEORGE PLIMPTON]. "Coda--'I'm not
     trying to be rosy about things like the atom bomb and war
     and the failure of the Presbyterian Church. Those things
     are awful'--William Styron," in The Idea of an American
     Novel. Edited by Louis D. Rubin, Jr., and John Rees Moore.
     New York: Thomas Y. Crowell, pp. 368-70.
          Excerpt from Styron's Paris Review interview, 1954.B3
     and 1958.B3.

18   MEEKER, RICHARD K. "The Youngest Generation of Southern Fic-
     tion Writers," in Southern Writers: Appraisals In Our Time.
     Edited by R. G. Simonini, Jr. Charlottesville: University
     of Virginia Press, pp. 162-91 [162-63, 171-73, 187-88].
          Examines Styron's view of Southern society in Lie Down
     in Darkness and views The Long March as a departure from
     Southern themes, a departure which is continued in Set This
     House on Fire.

19   MILLER, KARL. "An American Revenger," The Observer (London)
     (19 February), p. 29.
          Although Styron "has several obvious skills," Set This
     House on Fire is "a disappointment and a cheat," principally
     because "Cass's redemption and sobriety...are impossible to
     accept, and the effort to discern whether or not Flagg is
     'evil' is more or less relinquished, like Leverett, well
     before the end."

20   O'BRIEN, E. D. "A Literary Lounger," Illustrated London News,
     238 (11 March), 412.
          Although "it is too long, and the central character is
     not of such proportions as to carry the weight of almost
     Aeschylean tragedy which Mr. Styron has laid upon him,"
     nonetheless Set This House on Fire is "of considerable mer-
     it," for Styron "has much to tell us about art and life,
     about the soul of America, and about post-war Italy."

21   PRICE, R. G. G. Review of Set This House on Fire, Punch, 240
     (15 March), 441-42.
          "Although it is not by any means a good novel, it has
     certainly got something, though, when I try to think what,
     I find the vaguer memory of virtues dissolving in the more
     precise memory of vices."

22   ROTH, PHILIP. "Writing American Fiction," Commentary, 31
     (March), 223-33 [232-33].
          American fiction has problems when survival becomes, in
     itself, one's raison d'être, as in Set This House on Fire.

1961

23   RUBIN, LOUIS D., JR. "An Artist in Bonds," <u>Sewanee Review</u>, 69
     (Winter), 174-79.
         Although Styron is "the most impressive writer of fic-
     tion of his generation," there is one structural flaw in
     <u>Set This House on Fire</u>: Cass and Peter, dramatically and
     psychologically, are "one and the same person."

24   _____, and ROBERT D. JACOBS, eds. <u>South: Modern Southern Lit-
     erature In Its Cultural Setting</u>. Garden City, N.Y.: Dou-
     bleday.
     Contents includes:
     Louis D. Rubin, Jr. "Introduction--Southern Writing and the
         Changing South," pp. 11-28 [14, 21-23, 25].
         Styron, especially in <u>Lie Down in Darkness</u>, along with
     Agee and others, represents recent "Southern" writing by
     virtue of his language, and his conception of man as a
     limited dependent being. The sense of "community-as-all"
     no longer characterizes the Southern novel.
     Frederick J. Hoffman. "The Sense of Place," pp. 60-75 [68].
         Examines Styron's use of setting in <u>Lie Down in Darkness</u>.
     Walter Sullivan. "The Continuing Renascence: Southern
         Fiction in the Fifties," pp. 376-91 [385, 388-89].
         Speaks tentatively of Styron's Southernness in <u>Lie Down
     in Darkness</u>, noting his sense of family and of the past,
     but observing that Styron, unlike many of his predeces-
     sors, is at home in the modern world.

25   SCOTT, PAUL. Review of <u>Set This House on Fire</u>, <u>New Statesman
     and Nation</u>, 61 (17 February), 270-71.
         "This book outraged my sense of proportion-in-the-novel.
     I thought I saw something really good going to seed."

26   TYNDAREUS. "Recent Fiction," <u>John O'London's</u>, 4 (23 February),
     218.
         In <u>Set This House on Fire</u>, Styron has "Salinger's per-
     ception, though non of his delicacy."

27   WALDMEIR, JOSEPH. "Quest Without Faith," <u>The Nation</u>, 193 (18
     November), 390-96.
         Styron, like many of his contemporaries, is a great nov-
     elist, not in the traditional sense, but in a broader sense.
     <u>Lie Down in Darkness</u> and <u>Set This House on Fire</u> are exam-
     ined in this context.

28   WYRICK, GREEN D. "Book Review," Emporia (Kan.) <u>Gazette</u> (25
     February), p. 4. This review also appeared in Larned (Kan.)
     <u>Daily Tiller & Toiler</u> (24 February); Wellington (Kan.) <u>Mon-
     itor-Press</u> (23 February).

44

Set This House on Fire "fails simply on its level of believability."

1962 A BOOKS - NONE

1962 B SHORTER WRITINGS

1   ANDREA. "Paris Report--All of a Sudden...," Washington (D.C.)
     Star (15 April), p. D 3.
        Brief mention of conference on Styron held by French
     critic Michel Mohrt at the American Cultural Center in Paris.

2   ANON. "New Fiction," London Times (5 April), p. 13.
        The Long March is "a sterile work"; Styron "knows how
     to touch raw contemporary nerves; but he offers no hint of
     a solution, projects no mood of courage or kindness."

3   ANON. "Famous Peninsula Writer Interviewed When Latest Book
     Published In France," Newport News (Va.) Daily Press (27
     May), p. 4-D.
        Excerpts from an English translation of Styron's inter-
     view with Madeleine Chapsal (see below, 1962.B14), which
     deals primarily with American literary critics and with the
     reception of Set This House on Fire.

4   ANON. "Accolade For Able Young Author," Newport News (Va.)
     Times-Herald (24 July), p. 6.
        Editorial praising Styron's Life magazine story on
     Faulkner's funeral.

5   ANON. "Styron Authors Life Story on Faulkner Rites," Newport
     News (Va.) Daily Press (24 July), pp. 1, 16.
        Account of and quotations from Styron's Life piece on
     Faulkner's funeral.

6   BAUDRILLARD, JEAN. "'La Proie des Flammes,'" Les Temps Mod-
     ernes, 17 (June), 1928-37.
        Review of French translation of Set This House on Fire.

7   BENSON, ALICE R. "Techniques in the Twentieth Century Novel
     For Relating the Particular to the Universal: Set This
     House on Fire," Papers of the Michigan Academy of Science,
     Arts and Letters, 47, pp. 587-94.
        Finds in Styron's novel "a constant awareness of a mul-
     tiplicity of frames of reference" and is particularly con-
     cerned with the relationship between Set This House on Fire
     and "Oedipus at Colonus."

1962

8   BONNICHON, ANDRÉ. "William Styron et le second oedipe,"
    Études, 315 (October), 94–103.
        Review of the French translation of Set This House on
    Fire.

9   BOURNIQUEL, CAMILLE. "De la difficulte d'être...américain,"
    Esprit, 30 (May), 818–24 [820–24].
        Review of the French translation of Set This House on
    Fire.

10 B[RIERRE], A[NNIE]. "William Styron à Paris," France U.S.A.,
    No. 158 (March), 2.
        Interview and review of Lie Down in Darkness and Set This
    House on Fire.

11 _____. "La Proie des Critiques," Les Nouvelles Littéraires,
    40 (22 March), 8.
        Styron is one of three writers interviewed; he comments
    on Faulkner, his novel-in-progress (Nat Turner), contempo-
    rary writers, and on his non-fiction writings.

12 BRYDEN, RONALD. "Time of War," The Spectator, No. 6980 (6
    April), 454.
        The Long March is "an almost flawless achievement." If
    Styron "writes nothing else as finished as this, he will
    have justified the claims made for him."

13 BUTOR, MICHEL. "Oedipus Americanus [Préface]," in La Proie
    des flammes [Set This House on Fire]. Translated by
    Maurice-Edgar Coindreau. Paris: Éditions Gallimard, pp.
    vii–xx.

14 C[HAPSAL], M[ADELEINE]. "Entretien," L'Express (8 March), pp.
    26–27.
        Interview in which Styron talks about the reception of
    Set This House on Fire, Faulkner, American literary critics,
    and about the American creative writer. For an English
    translation of this piece, see 1962.B3.
    Reprinted: 1963.B7.

15 CHEYER, A. H. "WLB Biography: William Styron," Wilson Library
    Bulletin, 36 (April), 691.
        Biographical note which summarizes the plots and de-
    scribes the critical receptions of Lie Down in Darkness,
    The Long March, and Set This House on Fire.

16 FULLER, EDMUND. Books With Men Behind Them. New York: Ran-
    dom House, pp. 9–10.

Set This House on Fire is hailed as a major step in the maturing of Styron's considerable powers.

17   GREEN, PETER. "Growing Up in Golders Green," London Daily Telegraph and Morning Post (6 April), p. 19.
      The Long March is "a taut, brilliantly written novella."

18   HASSAN, IHAB. "The Character of Post-War Fiction in America," English Journal, 51 (January), 1-8 [2, 4, 7].
      Lie Down in Darkness and Set This House on Fire are cited as exemplifying the "energy of opposition" which is the energy of the contemporary novel. The Oedipal theme in Lie Down in Darkness and the existential theme in Set This House on Fire are also discussed.

19   HUGHES, DAVID. "Well Worth the Effort," London Sunday Times (8 April), p. 32.
      The Long March is "a sweaty physical book, but tender beneath it all, but violent, but thoughtful, but racy, but almost everything, and it acts on the mind with the swift completeness of a purge. Take it as soon as you can."

20   JUIN, HUBERT. "Rencontre avec William Styron," Les Lettres Françaises (1-8 March), p. 5.
      Interview in which Styron discusses Set This House on Fire, Faulkner, the South, and point of view in literature.

21   KAZIN, ALFRED. "The Alone Generation," in his Contemporaries. Boston: Little, Brown, pp. 214-16.
      Reprinting of Kazin's Harper's article, 1959.B6.

22   LAS VERGNAS, RAYMOND. "Étoiles Anglo-Américaines: Nathanael West, William Styron, Robert Penn Warren, Carson McCullers, V. Sackville-West," Les Annales (August), p. 33.

23   LAWSON, LEWIS. "Cass Kinsolving: Kierkegaardian Man of Despair," Wisconsin Studies in Contemporary Literature, 3 (Fall), 54-66.
      Only when Cass is viewed as a Kierkegaardian man of despair does his life take on enough significance to justify its very full presentation.

24   LE CLEC'H, GUY. "Un 'grand' de la nouvelle vague américaine: William Styron," Le Figaro Littéraire (24 February), p. 3.
      Interview in which Styron talks about the South and Set This House on Fire.

1962

25   LeMAIRE, MARCEL. "Some Recent American Novels and Essays," Revue des Langues Vivantes, 28 (January-February), 70-78 [72-74].
     In Set This House on Fire, Styron demonstrates that he is "a born writer but a confused one and the intensity of the writing is often too artificial, the result of an inflated style, a piling on of hyperbole and adjectives."

26   LUDWIG, JACK. Recent American Novelists. University of Minnesota Pamphlets on American Writers, No. 22. Minneapolis: University of Minnesota Press, pp. 31-34.
     Observes in Lie Down in Darkness and Set This House on Fire a theme "little different from the standard Beat lament; but Styron's fiction also contains a relieving glimpse of a Southern style that once was, and a human joy that might be."

27   McNAMARA, EUGENE. "The Post-Modern American Novel," Queen's Quarterly, 69 (Summer), 265-75.
     In technique and theme, Styron is one of those few writers "creating works which are original in a radical sense." Styron's characters in his three novels to date are all searching for authority.

28   MOHRT, MICHEL. "Les Trois Obsessions de William Styron: Le péché, le désespoir, le désir d'évasion," Arts (Paris), No. 858 (28 February-6 March), 3.
     Interview in which Styron talks about Set This House on Fire, Nat Turner, and his French translator, Maurice-Edgar Coindreau.

29   _____. "William Styron: 'J'écris l'histoire d'un illuminé qui tuait par devoir,'" Nouveau Candide, No. 70 (29 August), 13.
     Interview in which Styron comments on the American reviews of Set This House on Fire, on his novel-in-progress (Nat Turner), on Flaubert, and on his having attended a dinner at the White House.

30   NICHOLS, LEWIS. "In and Out of Books," New York Times Book Review (15 April), p. 8.
     Paragraph on Styron's current popularity and celebrity in France following publication there of Set This House on Fire.

31   ROSENTHAL, JEAN. "William Styron," Informations et Documents, No. 158 (15 March), 24.

32   RUBIN, LOUIS D., JR. "The South and the Faraway Country,"
      Virginia Quarterly Review, 38 (Summer), 444-59 [449].
           Lie Down in Darkness is cited as one version of the
      "young Southerner adrift in the metropolis" theme in an es-
      say on the Southern writer's relationship to his homeland.
      Reprinted: 1963.B22.

33   SLAVITT, DAVID R. "Poetry, Novels, and Critics: A Reply,"
      Yale Review, 51 (March), 502-504.
           Mentions Sytron briefly in essay contending that poets
      and novelists are facing similar problems.

1963 A BOOKS - NONE

1963 B SHORTER WRITINGS

1   ANON. "Professor and Writers," Duke Alumni Register, 49
      (April), 10-11.
           Four photographs and short text describing party given
      by Duke Professor William Blackburn for the Sytrons and
      some of Blackburn's present writing students.

2   ANON. "Our Own 'Impulse Toward Excellence,'" Charlotte News
      (24 April), p. 10A.
           Editorial on the occasion of the publication of Under
      Twenty-Five--Duke Narrative and Verse, 1945-1962, edited
      by Styron's former teacher, William Blackburn, and includ-
      ing an introductory essay by Styron. Styron is cited as
      one Blackburn student who has achieved national prominence.

3   ARNAVON, CYRILLE. "Les Romans de William Styron," Europe, 41
      (September), 54-66.

4   BRADBURY, JOHN M. Renaissance in the South: A Critical His-
      tory of the Literature, 1920-1960. Chapel Hill: Univer-
      sity of North Carolina Press, pp. 122-23 and passim.
           Styron seen as representing the new semi-existentialist
      leaning of the post-World War II generation of writers. In
      Lie Down in Darkness and Set This House on Fire, he writes
      about a new "lost generation" whose major problem has be-
      come suicide or the willful seeking of death.

5   BREADY, JAMES H. "About Books and Authors," Baltimore Sunday
      Sun (24 March), Sec. A, p. 5.
           Account of Styron's guest appearance in Elliott Coleman's
      writing seminar at Johns Hopkins University. Emphasis is

1963

on Mrs. Styron's Baltimore background and on Styron's own
associations with the city.

6   BRYANT, JERRY H. "The Hopeful Stoicism of William Styron,"
     South Atlantic Quarterly, 62 (Autumn), 539-50.
          Styron seen as giving progressively more mature answers
     to his central question--"What must man endure?"--in Lie
     Down in Darkness, The Long March, and Set This House on
     Fire.

7   CHAPSAL, MADELEINE. "William Styron," in her Quinze écrivains.
     Paris: René Julliard, pp. 173-81.
          Reprint of L'Express interview, 1962.B14.

8   DAVIS, ROBERT GORHAM. "The American Individualist Tradition:
     Bellow and Styron," in The Creative Present: Notes on Con-
     temporary Fiction. Edited by Nona Balakian and Charles
     Simmons. Garden City, N.Y.: Doubleday, pp. 111-41 [111-12,
     130-41].
          Styron and Bellow both exemplify "strong and explicit
     faith in the American individualist tradition." Lie Down
     in Darkness, The Long March, and, especially, Set This
     House on Fire are examined.
          Styron is also briefly discussed on pp. 197, 199, and
     212 of this collection of essays.

9   DOAR, HARRIET. "Styron: 'Human Being in Conflict,'" Charlotte
     Observer (24 March), p. 4-D.
          Interview in which Styron comments on the reception of
     Set This House on Fire, on the Paris Review, on Salinger
     and Updike, and on his novel-in-progress (Nat Turner).

10   _____. "Southern Writing: He's For It," Charlotte Observer
     (9 June), p. 17-A.
          Interview with publisher-author Hiram Haydn who calls
     Styron "'one of the two or three finest--maybe the finest--
     of his generation.'"

11   GALLOWAY, DAVID D. "The Absurd Hero in Contemporary Fiction:
     The Works of John Updike, William Styron, Saul Bellow, and
     J.D. Salinger." Ph.D. dissertation, University of Buffalo,
     1962 [Abstracted in Dissertation Abstracts, 23 (May), 4356-
     57].
          Examines variations in the quest for order and meaning
     in contemporary American fiction. Notes similarities and
     differences between the absurd man as Camus envisioned him
     and the fictional heroes studied as a critical aid to the

novelists' vision. This material, somewhat revised, appears
as 1965.B7 and 1966.B6.

12 HARTT, JULIAN. The Lost Image of Man. Baton Rouge: Louisiana
State University Press, pp. 60-63.
Lie Down in Darkness discussed briefly as marking the
"descent of erotic man into damnation all too palpable."

13 HOFFMAN, FREDERICK J. "Marginal Societies and the Contemporary
American Novel," in his The Modern Novel in America. Third
edition. Chicago: Henry Regnery, pp. 225-56 [239].
Styron in Lie Down in Darkness and Set This House on Fire
seen as motivated by a need to discover and define guilt.
Calls Styron's work "brilliant in its extravagant extensions
of passion" and expresses opinion that it will mature in the
future.

14 JOHANSSON, ERIC. "Lettres: les sortiléges de la mauvaise conscience," Démocratie (27 June), p. 10.

15 KLOTZ, MARVIN. "The Triumph Over Time: Narrative Form in
William Faulkner and William Styron," Mississippi Quarterly,
17 (Winter), 9-20.
Discusses Styron's "skillful subordination of chronology
to aesthetic demands" in Lie Down in Darkness and Set This
House on Fire. Styron structures his novels according to
the "climactic quality of his material." The structural
handlings of time in Faulkner and Styron are contrasted.

16 LAND, MYRICK. "Mr. Norman Mailer Challenges All the Talent in
the Room," in his The Fine Art of Literary Mayhem--A Lively
Account of Famous Writers and Their Feuds. New York: Holt,
Rinehart and Winston, pp. 216-38 [219, 221, 228].
Brief mention of Mailer's views on Styron's fiction.

17 MAILER, NORMAN. "Norman Mailer vs. Nine Writers," Esquire, 60
(July), 63-69, 105.
Set This House on Fire dismissed as "overblown uncon-
ceived philosophy."

18 MITCHELL, RICHARD. "An Age of Issues and a Literature of Trou-
bles," Western Humanities Review, 17 (Autumn), 349-60 [352].
Examines the blurring effect of literary tradition on
such modern writers as Styron, Bellow, Updike, and Salinger.

19 M[OHRT], M[ICHEL]. "Note du Traducteur," in La marche de nuit
[The Long March]. Translated by Michel Mohrt. Paris:

1963

Éditions Gallimard, pp. 7-9.
Brief history of the novel's composition.

20   NOGGLE, BURT. "Variety and Ambiguity: The Recent Approach to
      Southern History," Mississippi Quarterly, 17 (Winter), 21-
      33 [33].
          In contrast to older Southern novelists, more recent nov-
      elists such as Styron and James Agee "have lost their sense
      of community, of involvement within a limited, boundless
      universe."

21   RAHV, PHILIP. "Introduction," in Eight Great American Short
      Novels. Edited by Philip Rahv. New York: Berkley, pp.
      9-17 [16-17].
          Brief analysis of The Long March (anthologized in this
      collection): it "impresses us not merely as an extraordi-
      narily vivid account of a physical ordeal but as a vehicle
      discovering and exploring a new theme, that of the rebellion
      of those 'born into a generation of conformists.'"

22   RUBIN, LOUIS D., JR. "William Styron: Notes on a Southern
      Writer in Our Time," in his The Faraway Country: Writers
      of the Modern South. Seattle: University of Washington
      Press, pp. 185-230.
          "The history of Styron's two novels [Lie Down in Darkness
      and Set This House on Fire] is closely tied in with what
      Southern literature has been during the past several years,
      and what it can and might be in the future." This book also
      reprints 1962.B32.
      Reprinted: 1975.A4.

23   ____. "The Difficulties of Being a Southern Writer Today,"
      Journal of Southern History, 29 (November), 486-94.
          A look at Styron's career reveals much of the history
      and many of the problems of Southern writers in general.
      Reprinted: 1967.B138.

24   ____. "An Interview With...William Styron," Hollins College
      Bulletin, 14 (November), 8-11.
          Styron comments on creative writing classes, Set This
      House on Fire, Faulkner, book reviewers, and first novels.

25   SEARS, ROBERT B. "Author Chides Critics--Reviewers Go Astray
      By 'Thinking': Styron," Roanoke Times (3 March), p. B-2.
          Account of Styron's talk about book reviewers delivered
      at Hollins College luncheon.

26 STEVENSON, DAVID L. "William Styron and the Fiction of the
    Fifties," in <u>Recent American Fiction: Some Critical Views</u>.
    Edited by Joseph L. Waldmeir. Boston: Houghton Mifflin,
    pp. 265-74.
        Reprint of Stevenson's <u>Critique</u> essay, 1960.B112.

27 _____. "The Activists," <u>Daedalus,</u> 92 (Spring), 238-49 [241].
        Observes that Styron's characters continue to exist as
    studies in moral responsibility as opposed to the "activ-
    ist" heroes of Bellow, Percy, and others.

28 TALESE, GAY. "Looking For Hemingway," <u>Esquire,</u> 60 (July), 44-
    47.
        Account of an evening at George Plimpton's with "the
    <u>Paris Review</u> crowd," including Styron, Mailer, James Jones,
    and others.

29 THOMPSON, F. H. "Hell Is Not Giving," <u>Prairie Schooner,</u> 37
    (Summer), 183-85.
        "It is hoped that Styron is talented enough and wise
    enough not to be fashionable for long."

1964 A BOOKS - NONE

1964 B SHORTER WRITINGS

1   ALDRIDGE, JOHN W. "Highbrow Authors and Middlebrow Books,"
    <u>Playboy,</u> 11 (April), 119, 166-74 [172-74].
        Styron's literary standards have unfortunately become
    too widely known and accepted to be very seriously consid-
    ered anymore, but he perfectly fulfills middlebrow expec-
    tations for serious literature without ever being uncom-
    fortably original. In <u>Set This House on Fire</u>, however, he
    may have gone too far for middlebrow tastes. For an ex-
    panded version of this essay, <u>see</u> 1966.B1 and 1972.B1.

2   ALLEN, WALTER. <u>The Modern Novel in Britain and the United</u>
    <u>States</u>. New York: E. P. Dutton, pp. 305-307.
        <u>Lie Down in Darkness</u> is seen as "one of the major novels
    of the decade" and an attempt at Freudian tragedy. The
    structure, themes, and Southern elements of the novel are
    discussed.

3   ANON. "Catch $95," <u>Newsweek,</u> 63 (9 March), 83-84.
        Styron comments on movies and novels in article which
    examines the trend toward novelist-screenwriters, specifi-
    cally Styron, Heller, and Terry Southern.

1964

4   BAUMBACH, JONATHAN. "Paradise Lost: The Novels of William
    Styron," South Atlantic Quarterly, 63 (Spring), 207-17.
         Lie Down in Darkness is seen as a "study of a paradise
    fallen into chaos, the end result of a romantic conception
    of morality." Set This House on Fire is "a symbolic pil-
    grimmage into hell in search of, of all things, the sight
    of God."
    Reprinted: 1965.B3.

5   DETWEILER, ROBERT. "William Styron and the Courage To Be,"
    in his Four Spiritual Crises in Mid-Century American Fic-
    tion. Gainesville: University of Florida Press, pp. 6-
    13.
         The vocabulary and sequence of spiritual events in Set
    This House on Fire echo Tillich and Kierkegaard; but Styron
    succeeds in making Cass' dilemma personal and not dogmatic.

6   DOAR, HARRIET. "Interview With William Styron," Red Clay
    Reader, 1, pp. 26-30.
         Styron talks about Southern writing, contemporary writ-
    ers, the sense of place in fiction, and about the relation-
    ship between social problems and writing.

7   GEISMAR, MAXWELL. "The American Short Story Today," Studies
    on the Left, 4 (Spring), 21-27 [26].
         Despite the predominance of short story writers who are
    preoccupied with psychological themes, Styron is one indi-
    cation that our best fiction is still based on the "real-
    istic-naturalistic premise."

8   GRESSET, MICHEL. "Sur William Styron," Mercure de France,
    350 (February), 297-303.

9   HASSAN, IHAB. "Encounter With Necessity: Three Novels By
    Styron, Swados, and Mailer," in On Contemporary Literature.
    Edited by Richard Kostelanetz. New York: Avon, pp. 597-
    606.
         Reprint of 1961.B12.

10 KOSTELANETZ, RICHARD. "The Bad Criticism of This Age," Min-
    nesota Review, 4 (Spring), 387-414 [391, 392, 393, 396,
    408].
         Contends that Jack Ludwig misses "the beauty of Styron's
    rhythmic, involuted, baroque prose"; but Hassan understands
    Styron's genius in Lie Down in Darkness. Rubin's work on
    Styron is seen as overly preoccupied with the agrarian
    theme.

11 MILLGATE, MICHAEL. American Social Fiction: James to
    Cozzens. New York: Barnes and Noble, p. 201.
        Recent American novelists, notably Bellow and Styron,
    remain self-conscious about their relations to society and
    often make an overly ambitious attempt to create and sus-
    tain the whole social area in which their characters move.

12 MUDRICK, MARVIN. "Mailer and Styron: Guests of the Estab-
    lishment," Hudson Review, 17 (Autumn), 346-66.
        Harsh indictment of Styron and his three novels to date.
    He is comfortable in Establishment drawing rooms by virtue
    of "talent, but not too vigorously exhibited; style without
    bite or intelligence; supine moralities momentarily illumi-
    nated by sulphur and brimstone."
    Reprinted: 1970.B15.

13 O'CONNOR, WILLIAM VAN. "John Updike and William Styron: The
    Burden of Talent," in Contemporary American Novelists. Ed-
    ited by Harry T. Moore. Carbondale: Southern Illinois
    University Press, pp. 205-21.
        In Styron's three novels to date there is "enormous tal-
    ent in search of a subject." Updike at least has something
    to write about.

14 PODHORETZ, NORMAN. "The Gloom of Philip Roth," in his Doings
    and Undoings. New York: Farrar, Straus, pp. 236-43 [240-
    42].
        Roth is bewildered by the affirmative tone of Set This
    House on Fire and other contemporary fiction, but his own
    stance (in Letting Go) is much less successful.

15 SCHICKEL, RICHARD. "The Old Criticism and the New Novel,"
    Wisconsin Studies in Contemporary Literature, 5 (Winter-
    Spring), 26-36.
        The novels of Styron and others are, but they stubbornly
    refuse to mean despite the intense, obvious effort which
    has gone into them. Styron is among those writers schooled
    in the library, but not in life.

16 SULLIVAN, WALTER. "The Decline of Regionalism in Southern
    Fiction," Georgia Review, 18 (Fall), 300-308 [306, 307].
        Styron is seen as cut off from his tradition and unable
    to find any other. He uses the South merely as a setting.
    Much of this material is reprinted in 1976.B11.

17 THORP, WILLARD. "The Southern Mode," South Atlantic Quarterly,
    63 (Autumn), 576-82 [578-79].
        Expresses doubt that Set This House on Fire is written
    in the "Southern mode."

1965

1965 A BOOKS

1   MILLS, HELEN SLABY. "An Examination of the Psychological
    Validity of Characters in Lie Down in Darkness." M.A.
    thesis, Sacramento State College.
        "It is my intention in this paper....to show that
    Styron's presentation is consistent with the Freudian psy-
    choanalytic viewpoint of Karl Menninger, M.D., noted psychi-
    atrist, as given in his book Man Against Himself (1938)."

2   SCOTT, JAMES B. "The Individual and Society: Norman Mailer
    Versus William Styron." Ph.D. dissertation, Syracuse Uni-
    versity, 1964 [Abstract in Dissertation Abstracts, 25
    (April), 5942].
        Studies the first three novels of each author, arguing
    that Mailer abandons society and extols the individual
    while Styron increasingly insists that the individual must
    conform to the limitations of society.

1965 B SHORTER WRITINGS

1   ANON. "American Fiction: The Postwar Years, 1945-1965," Book
    Week (New York Herald Tribune, Washington Post, Chicago
    Sun-Times, San Francisco Examiner) (26 September).
        Special issue of Book Week which includes Styron as one
    of twenty who have "written the most distinguished fiction
    during the period 1945-65" (p. 3), lists Lie Down in Dark-
    ness as one of the twenty best books of the period selected
    through a poll (p. 5), and quotes Walter Allen (p. 7) and
    Carlos Fuentes (p. 20) with praise for Styron. See also
    1972.B10.

2   BAKER, ROBERT E. LEE. "Looking at Dixie 100 Years Later,"
    Washington Post (10 April), p. A12.
        Brief mention of Styron's piece, "This Quiet Dust," in
    April issue of Harper's.

3   BAUMBACH, JONATHAN. "Paradise Lost: Lie Down in Darkness By
    William Styron," in his The Landscape of Nightmare: Studies
    in the Contemporary Novel. New York: New York University
    Press, pp. 123-37.
        Reprint of Baumbach's South Atlantic Quarterly essay,
    1964.B4. See also 1961.B5.

4   BLATCHFORD, EDWARD. "William Styron at Yale--Four Hours of
    Questions," Yale Daily News (8 January), p. 1.
        Brief account of Styron's informal remarks to Yale stu-
    dent audience.

5   DOMMERGUES, PIERRE. "L'ambiguité de l'innocence," <u>Langues</u>
    <u>Modernes</u>, 59 (March-April), 54-59.

6   FINKELSTEIN, SIDNEY. "Cold War, Religious Revival, and Family
    Alienation: William Styron, J.D. Salinger and Edward Albee,"
    in his <u>Existentialism and Alienation in American Literature</u>.
    New York: International Publishers, pp. 211-42 [215-19, 223].
        <u>Lie Down in Darkness</u>, <u>The Long March</u>, and <u>Set This House</u>
    <u>on Fire</u> are discussed. Unlike Faulkner, Styron treats his
    characters' problems as purely subjective and proves to be
    an excellent psychologist.

7   GALLOWAY, DAVID. "The Absurd Man as Tragic Hero," <u>Texas Stud-</u>
    <u>ies in Literature and Language</u>, 6 (Winter), 512-34.
        Styron's three novels to date are examined in terms of
    Camus' Myth of Sisyphus. In <u>Set This House on Fire</u>, an af-
    firmation of the order of the universe is achieved, through
    the attempted creation of a tragic hero. Much of this ma-
    terial appeared in Galloway's dissertation, 1963.B11.
    Reprinted: 1966.B6.

8   GOSSETT, LOUISE Y. "The Cost of Freedom: William Styron,"
    in her <u>Violence in Recent Southern Fiction</u>. Durham, N.C.:
    Duke University Press, pp. 117-31.
        Styron's characters try to establish "a creative rela-
    tion between freedom and discipline." The cost of this at-
    tempt is "frustration, jealousy, betrayal, despair, and
    death," as seen in his three novels to date.

9   GRIFFIN, JACK, JERRY HOMSY, and GENE STELZIG. "A Conversation
    With William Styron," <u>The Handle</u> (University of Pennsylva-
    ia), 2 (Spring), 16-29.
        Styron reviews his career and comments on his novels, on
    the influence of Faulkner on his work, and on critics.

10 HASSAN, IHAB. "The Novel of Outrage: A Minority Voice in
    Postwar American Fiction," <u>American Scholar</u>, 34 (Spring),
    239-53 [243-44].
        <u>Set This House on Fire</u> exemplifies "the ambiguous novel
    of outrage." It brings us "artificially close to the facts
    of violence," but ends by evading them.

11 HAYS, PETER L. "The Nature of Rebellion in <u>The Long March</u>,"
    <u>Critique</u> (Minneapolis), 8 (Winter), 70-74.
        Styron does not lament or applaud Mannix, but he does
    provide him with a mythological and literary heritage de-
    scended from Prometheus, Satan, old Adam, and Jesus--all
    representatives of indomitable will in spite of pain and
    suffering.

1965

*12   KRZECZKOWSKI, HENRYK. Untitled note, in Pogrążyć się w mroku
       [Lie Down in Darkness]. Warsaw: Państwowy Instytut
       Wydawniczy, pp. 560-64.
          West, Item H 45.

13   MOORE, L. HUGH. "Robert Penn Warren, William Styron, and the
       Use of Greek Myth," Critique (Minneapolis), 8 (Winter), 75-
       87.
          Believes that Styron envisioned Set This House on Fire as
       a Greek tragedy concerned with "modern America's desperate
       need for catharsis."

14   O'CONNELL, SHAUN. "Expense of Spirit: The Vision of William
       Styron," Critique (Minneapolis), 8 (Winter), 20-33.
          Examines Styron's three novels to date as "a stylistically
       interrelated and thematically unified body of fiction."
       Styron's vision, introduced in Lie Down in Darkness, is most
       fully explored in Set This House on Fire.

15   OPPENHEIMER, MARTIN. Letter to the Editor, Harper's Magazine,
       230 (June), 8.
          Disputes Styron's contention, in "This Quiet Dust" (Harp-
       er's, April 1965), that there were only three uprisings in
       the history of American slavery. For Styron's reply to this
       letter, see West, Item F 10.

16   ROBB, KENNETH A. "William Styron's Don Juan," Critique (Min-
       neapolis), 8 (Winter), 34-46.
          The Don Juan legend via Mozart via Kierkegaard informs
       Set This House on Fire with a coherence and unity that cor-
       relates well with Styron's depiction of Cass as a "Kierke-
       gaardian man of despair," as seen by Lawson, 1962.B24.
       Reprinted: 1970.B18.

17   RUBIN, LOUIS D., JR. "Notes on the Literary Scene: Their Own
       Language," Harper's Magazine, 230 (April), 173-75 [174].
          Sees in Styron's work attitudes being questioned which
       were implicitly accepted by Faulkner.

18   de SAINT PHALLE, THÉRÈSE. "William Styron (Heritier Littéraire
       de Faulkner)," Le Figaro Littéraire (1-7 July), p. 16.
          Interview in which Styron talks of his novel-in-progress
       (Nat Turner), of the South, and of his writing habits.

19   URANG, GUNNAR. "The Broader Vision: William Styron's Set This
       House on Fire," Critique (Minneapolis), 8 (Winter), 47-69.
          Sees the book's weaknesses as inherent in Styron's com-
       plex task. Interprets the affirmative movement of the nov-
       el as constituting "a Christian pattern of redemption."

1966 A BOOKS

1   NIGRO, AUGUST. "William Styron and the Adamic Tradition."
    Ph.D. dissertation, University of Maryland, 1964 [Abstract-
    ed in Dissertation Abstracts, 26 (January), 3958-59].
        Observes in Styron's three novels to date the encounter
    between a fallen or doomed Adam and a hostile world. This
    results in the withdrawal of the disillusioned Adam, "fixed
    in adolescent lament" in favor of a wiser, more mature hero.
    Some of this material is reprinted in 1967.A1.

1966 B SHORTER WRITINGS

1   ALDRIDGE, JOHN W. "William Styron and the Derivative Imagina-
    tion," in his Time to Murder and Create: The Contemporary
    Novel in Crisis. New York: David McKay, pp. 30-51; also
    pp. 72, 91-93.
        Styron's principal weakness in Lie Down in Darkness and
    Set This House on Fire is a middlebrow one. He has not
    found it possible "to operate outside the system of ideolo-
    gical and dramatic conventions that have become the clichés
    of the highbrow world even as they remain the intellectual
    status symbols of the middlebrow world." Some of this ma-
    terial appeared originally in Aldridge's Playboy essay,
    1964.B1.
    Reprinted: 1972.B1.

2   ANON. "Another Honor For a Native Son," Newport News (Va.)
    Daily Press (7 February), p. 4.
        Editorial hailing Styron's recent election to the Na-
    tional Institute of Arts and Letters.

3   CANZONERI, ROBERT, and PAGE STEGNER. "An Interview With
    William Styron," Per/Se, 1 (Summer), 37-44.
        Styron talks of his longtime interest in Nat Turner, of
    Nat Turner as religious allegory and as a psychological
    novel; and he outlines the plot of Nat Turner.

4   CARVER, WAYNE. "The Grand Inquisitor's Long March," Denver
    Quarterly, 1 (Summer), 37-64.
        Styron's The Long March and Dostoevski's The Legend
    of the Grand Inquisitor are examined in a broad social con-
    text. Styron's novel is about "the practical futility of
    rebellion" within a system in which "efficiency and order
    are ends in themselves."

1966

5   FRIEDMAN, MELVIN J. "The Cracked Vase," Romance Notes, 7
    (Spring), 127-29.
        Sees Styron using a metaphor used by Stendhal in Le Rouge
    et le noir: when he breaks a vase, Cass catches "a reveal-
    ing glimpse into his future."

6   GALLOWAY, DAVID D. "The Absurd Man as Tragic Hero" and "A
    William Sytron Checklist," in his The Absurd Hero in Amer-
    ican Fiction. Austin: University of Texas Press, pp. 51-
    81 and 208-20.
        The chapter on Styron is a reprinting of Galloway's Tex-
    as Studies essay, 1965.B7, which in turn is a reworking of
    material from Galloway's dissertation, 1963.B11. The check-
    list is largely unannotated.

7   HUX, SAMUEL H. "American Myth and Existential Vision: The
    Indigenous Existentialism of Mailer, Bellow, Styron, and
    Ellison." Ph.D. dissertation, University of Connecticut
    [Abstracted in Dissertation Abstracts, 26 (March), 5437].
        Notes the differences between American and European ex-
    istentialism. Since American existentialism grows out of
    the failure of the Edenic myth, it is still nourished by
    myth. Alienation for these American novelists is histori-
    cal and not ontological.

*8 ISTVÁN, HERMANN. Untitled note, in Házam Lángra Gyullad [Set
    This House on Fire]. Budapest: Európa Könyvkiadó, pp.
    561-71.
        West, Item H 25.

9   KELLY, FREDERIC. "William Styron Tells the Story of the Nat
    Turner Rebellion," New Haven Register (14 August), Sunday
    Pictorial Section, pp. 7-9.
        Interview in which Styron speaks of his forthcoming
    novel--how he wrote it and its themes.

10 KING, LARRY L. "The Ole Country Boys," Texas Observer, 58 (24
    June), 10-12.
        Account of visit to home of writer-editor Willie Morris
    and party which Styron attended. Includes brief Styron
    comment on writing.

11 SACHS, VIOLA. "Contemporary American Fiction and Some Nine-
    teenth Century Patterns," Kwartalnik Neofilogizny, 13 (First
    Quarter), 3-29 [6-7, 15-16, 27-28].
        Set This House on Fire depicts rootlessness, nostalgia
    for the past, the failure of the American dream--themes

initiated by nineteenth-century American writers such as
Cooper, Hawthorne, Melville, and Twain.

12   WALCUTT, CHARLES CHILD.   "Idea Marching On One Leg," in his
      Man's Changing Mask: Modes and Methods of Characterization
      in Fiction. Minneapolis: University of Minnesota Press,
      pp. 251-57.
           The Long March is about the alienation and masochism of
      the Jew in the person of Mannix. Characterization and prob-
      ability suffer; the idea is too big for the story.

1967 A BOOKS

1   FRIEDMAN, M[ELVIN] J., and A[UGUST] J. NIGRO, eds. Configu-
     ration Critique de William Styron. Paris: Minard-Lettres
     Modernes, 152 pp.
     Contents:
     Melvin J. Friedman. "Préface," pp. 7-31.
          Expanded version, in French, of Friedman's English Jour-
     nal essay, 1961.B9.
     Frederick J. Hoffman. "La Thérapeutique du Néant--Les
     Romans de William Styron," pp. 33-56.
          For an English translation of this essay, see 1967.B77.
     See also 1968.B76.
     David L. Stevenson. "L'Individu, Le Milieu et La Liberté
     Dans Les Romans de William Styron," pp. 57-71.
     Roger Asselineau. "En Suivant La Marche de Nuit," pp. 73-
     83.
     Melvin J. Friedman. "William Styron et le Nouveau Roman,"
     pp. 85-109.
          For an English translation of this essay, see 1972.B8;
     and 1974.A2.
     August J. Nigro. "Murir a Sambuco," pp. 111-21.
     James Boatwright. "Réflexions sur Styron, ses Critiques et
     ses Sources," pp. 123-35.
     August J. Nigro. "William Styron--Sélection Bibliographi-
     que," pp. 137-51.
          Unannotated listing of works by and about Styron.

1967 B SHORTER WRITINGS

1   ANCRUM, CALHOUN. "Novel By Styron Gets Rave Notices," Charles-
     ton (S.C.) News and Courier (31 December), p. 2-D.
          The Confessions of Nat Turner is "the masterpiece of all
     American prose."

1967

2 ANON. Review of <u>The Confessions of Nat Turner</u>, <u>Publishers'</u>
   <u>Weekly</u>, 192 (31 July), 53.
       Though <u>The Confessions of Nat Turner</u> "is a novel of the
   oppressed human spirit, it is rescued from total depres-
   sion by Mr. Styron's storytelling skill."

3 ANON. Review of <u>The Confessions of Nat Turner</u>, <u>Kirkus</u>, 35 (1
   August), 905.
       It is a book "uneasy to reconcile--whether as a polemic
   or a novel....There is no correspondence between the Nat
   Turner who lived and died before the Civil War and the Nat
   Turner who seems to be a superimposition of the 60's res-
   urrected in some flagrantly modern scenes."

4 ANON. "A Correction," New York <u>Times</u> (7 August), p. 27.
       Notes that Random House is publisher of <u>Nat Turner</u>, not
   Viking Press, as reported in earlier article by Alden
   Whitman, 1967.B170.

5 ANON. "Nat Turner Book Tells of Rebels," New York <u>Amsterdam</u>
   <u>News</u> (2 September), p. 5.
       Pre-publication blurb based on <u>Esquire</u> excerpt from <u>Nat</u>
   <u>Turner</u>.

6 ANON. "In the Book World," Chicago's <u>American</u> (8 October),
   Sec. 3, p. 5.
       "Styron, in fictionalizing the Nat Turner story, has
   produced a grim, moving, masterful novel."

7 ANON. "The Idea of Hope," <u>Time</u>, 90 (13 October), 110, 113.
       In <u>The Confessions of Nat Turner</u>, "Styron's narrative
   power, lucidity and understanding of the epoch of slavery
   achieve a new peak in the literature of the South."

8 ANON. "The Novelist as a Rebel Slave," <u>Life</u>, 63 (13 October),
   51-52, 54.
       Picture-story on Styron and <u>Nat Turner</u>, followed by ex-
   cerpt from the novel (pp. 54-60).

9 ANON. "The World of Nat Turner," Boston <u>Sunday Globe</u> (22 October), p. 4-A.
       Editorial praising <u>Nat Turner</u>: the book is "a creative
   achievement on a par with" <u>The Red Badge of Courage</u>.

10 ANON. "Howe and Styron to Write Book Column for Harper's,"
    New York <u>Times</u> (26 October), p. 40.
        Irving Howe and Styron will alternate writing a book
    column for <u>Harper's</u>, beginning in January 1968.

11   ANON. Review of The Confessions of Nat Turner, Playboy, 14
      (November), 32.
          As a novel, it "has obvious weaknesses: It is a one-
      character book; its arguments sometimes verge on the sim-
      plistic; and it is occasionally dull. But even with these
      faults, there has been no better book of fiction this year."

12   ANON. Review of The Confessions of Nat Turner, America, 117
      (25 November), 666.
          "Mr. Styron has fulfilled the promise critics have been
      seeing in him."

13   ANON. "Ebony Book Shelf," Ebony, 23 (December), 20.
          Brief descriptive review of The Confessions of Nat
      Turner.

14   ANON. Review of The Confessions of Nat Turner, Booklist, 64
      (1 December), 425.
          Brief descriptive review.

15   APTHEKER, HERBERT. "Styron--Turner and Nat Turner: Myth and
      Truth," Political Affairs, 46 (October), 40-50.
          Examines "Styron's distortion of the historical Nat
      Turner." The novel represents the fictional embodiment of
      the Stanley Elkins school of thought on **slavery**, the idea
      that "Sambos" were the product of enslavement.

16   _____. "A Note on the History," The Nation, 205 (16 October),
      375-76.
          Styron's departures from the historical realities of the
      Nat Turner rebellion are numerous and serious; they are part
      of "a distortion widespread in the United States at the pre-
      sent time."
      Reprinted: 1970.A1; 1971.A2.

17   ARNELL, DAVE. "Styron on 'Nat Turner'--Novelist Says 'Love'
      May Be Path to Racial Peace," Springfield (Ohio) Sun (22
      November), pp. 1, 4.
          Account of Styron lecture at Wilberforce University.

18   ARTOPOEUS, JOHN B. "'A Meditation on History,'" Newark (N.J.)
      Sunday News (8 October), Sec. 1, p. A6.
          Although Styron "has done superbly in creating his hero,"
      once "the book is closed Turner is still just Styron's
      creation."

19   BARKHAM, JOHN. "Sixty Whites Were Killed in 1831 Slave Riots,"
      Youngstown Vindicator (8 October), p. 12-B. This syndicated

review also appeared in Woodland (Calif.) <u>Democrat</u> (18 October); Lewiston (Idaho) <u>Tribune</u> (15 October); Albany (N.Y.) <u>Times-Union</u> (8 October); Waukegan (Ill.) <u>News Sun</u> (7 October); Grand Rapids (Mich.) <u>Press</u> (8 October).
    <u>The Confessions of Nat Turner</u> is a "somber, deeply felt achievement by a writer whose heart and art have both been involved."

20   BAUER, MALCOLM. "Swords That Made 'Sore Slaughter,'" Portland <u>Sunday Oregonian</u> (15 October), p. F3.
    Anyone who reads <u>The Confessions of Nat Turner</u> "will not forget this episode in American history or the national tragedy it symbolizes."

21   BENKE, DICK. "Plight of Negro Slaves Mirrored By Nat Turner," Pasadena (Calif.) <u>Independent Star News</u> (15 October), p. B8.
    <u>The Confessions of Nat Turner</u> is "a beautifully written, beautifully constructed, lyrical, truthful, simple, direct literary masterpiece [which]....will survive long after racial bigotry has vanished...."

22   BICKHAM, JACK M. "Truth Hurts," Oklahoma City <u>Sunday Oklahoman</u> (8 October), Sec. 1, p. 28.
    "No one's platitudes or self-deceptions can really stand before this kind of story, if the story is honestly faced."

23   BILLINGS, CLAUDE. "'Confessions' Bares Negro Slave Revolt," Indianapolis <u>Star</u> (17 December), Sec. 8, p. 7.
    With <u>The Confessions of Nat Turner</u>, Styron is "back in the top bracket of American novelists and will give contemporaries some keen competition for best novel of 1967."

24   BIRDSELL, ROGER. "The Reading Lamp: Styron's Black Hamlet," South Bend <u>Tribune</u> (15 October), Sec. 1, p. 16.
    <u>The Confessions of Nat Turner</u> is "more than an intellectual achievement. Nat Turner is as timeless as Hamlet, another feat of historical imagination transcending the time and place of his creator."

25   BLACK, KAY PITTMAN. "Agonies of Slavery Recounted in Novel About Nat Turner," Memphis <u>Press-Scimitar</u> (22 September), p. 6.
    <u>The Confessions of Nat Turner</u> is "an important book for Southerners and all Americans to read if they have a hard time understanding today's Negro and his constant references to slavedom past and the recent slavedom present of token desegregation, no admittance signs and little pay."

26   BRADLEY, VAN ALLEN. "Styron Tells Slave's Saga," Memphis <u>Com-</u>
     <u>mercial Appeal</u> (15 October), Sec. 5, p. 6. This syndicated
     review also appeared in Birmingham (Ala.) <u>News</u> (15 October);
     Chicago <u>Daily News</u> (7 October); Albany (N.<u>Y.</u>) <u>Knickerbocker-</u>
     <u>News</u> (14 October).
         <u>The Confessions of Nat Turner</u> is "a triumph of daring
     design and execution."

27   BRANDRIFF, WELLES T. "The Role of Order and Disorder in <u>The</u>
     <u>Long March</u>," <u>English Journal</u>, 56 (January), 54-59.
         Styron's novel deals with "the thin, fabricated veneer
     called civilization, and one man's growing awareness of the
     essential disorder which lies just beneath the surface of
     this veneer." The symbolism and sound motif of the novel
     are examined in light of this theme.

28   BUCKMASTER, HENRIETTA. "Racism, 1831: The Fire Last Time,"
     <u>Christian Science Monitor</u> (12 October), p. 5.
         <u>The Confessions of Nat Turner</u> "is not a novel for the
     squeamish, but if the reader can stay his course he will
     find that a blazing light has been shed on dark corners."

29   BUNKE, JOAN. "Styron Novel Is Powerful as Fiction and Sermon,"
     Des Moines <u>Register</u> (15 October), p. 7-T.
         <u>The Confessions of Nat Turner</u> is "a moving achievement,
     a triumph of fictional characterization and a sermon--though
     Styron specifically denies a preachment--on the evils of
     dooming a man to a false image."

30   BUTCHER, FANNY. Review of <u>The Confession of Nat Turner</u>,
     Chicago <u>Tribune</u> (25 October), Sec. 1, p. 22.
         <u>The Confessions of Nat Turner</u> "is a literary tour de
     force which achieves the almost impossible task of a white
     man living inside the heart and the mind and the skin of a
     black slave."

31   C., S. J. "Styron's Search For One Man's Soul," Baltimore <u>News</u>
     <u>American</u> (8 October), p. 2G.
         "In his own attempt to know the Negro, the author has
     written a beautiful novel, one that will provoke discussion,
     argument and, maybe, thought."

32   CLEMONS, JOEL. "Author Dramatizes Event Masterfully," Charles-
     ton (S.C.) <u>News and Courier</u> (31 December), p. 2-D.
         <u>The Confessions of Nat Turner</u> "will undoubtedly emerge
     as a major work in American contemporary literature."

1967

33 COLE, VERNE. "Novel of Revolt," Fresno Bee (12 November), p. 17-F.
"The story of Turner and the revolt is well worth telling and Styron tells it well."

34 COLLIER, PETER. "Saga of Rebellion," The Progressive, 31 (December), 41-42.
The "intersection of historical and human crisis" makes The Confessions of Nat Turner "a novel of major importance."

35 COLLINS, L. M. "Exam: Don't Flunk It!" Nashville Tennessean (1 October), p. 6-B.
Descriptive review of The Confessions of Nat Turner.

36 COMINSKY, J. R., and ELIZABETH HARDWICK. "Reading Around the World," London Sunday Times (31 December), p. 22.
In survey of year's publications in different countries, both Cominsky and Hardwick--in separate pieces--mention Nat Turner as among the year's most important books.

37 COOK, BRUCE. "Fiction Verifies the Facts of a Tidewater Tale," National Observer (9 October), p. 22.
The "triumph" of The Confessions of Nat Turner is "that we can learn the bitter lesson of history that is there for us without having it lectured."

38 COYLE, WILLIAM. "A Major American Novel," Springfield (Ohio) Sun (28 October), Sec. 1, p. 6.
As "a social document," The Confessions of Nat Turner "is so painfully relevant that it is easy to exaggerate its excellence as a literary work. A hundred years from now it may seem a rather ordinary novel whose timeliness aroused the conscience of its time. Just now it seems one of the major American novels of the century."

39 CUNNINGHAM, DICK. "Styron Writes of Negro With Inside-Out View," Minneapolis Tribune (8 October), p. 6-E.
In The Confessions of Nat Turner, "the conclusion is foregone but the tension is almost tangible."

40 CURRIE, EDWARD. "Author William Styron--Era's Clarion," Rocky Mountain News (Denver) (22 October), Startime Section, p. 19.
The Confessions of Nat Turner contains "compelling eloquence, and forceful even powerful narrative."

41 DAVIS, PAXTON. "Mr. Styron and His Nat Turner," Roanoke Times (29 October), p. D7.

In The Confessions of Nat Turner, Styron's "intention is always serious and his aim high--he never stoops to the cheap effect and, despite the pretentious claim of his preface, he works hard at bringing the reality of his subject home."

42 DERLETH, AUGUST. "Books of the Times--Wm Styron's Fourth Novel," Capital Times (Madison, Wis.) (19 October), Sec. 1, p. 27.
    Styron is not totally successful at creating "a character who holds the reader's sympathy throughout the book"; but The Confessions of Nat Turner is "a tour de force."

43 DIXON, DONALD C. Review of The Confessions of Nat Turner, Reading Guide (University of Virginia Law School), 23 (December), 1-3.
    The "central impact" of The Confessions of Nat Turner "lies in the meaning of anguish and in a chilling exposition of the psychology of hatred and vengeance."

44 DUBERMAN, MARTIN. "Books," Village Voice (14 December), pp. 8-9.
    "In adhering to the historical Nat Turner, Styron has had to renounce those rich powers of invention which make his secondary characters so memorable."
    Reprinted: 1969.B10.

45 DUFFER, KEN. "Styron Recovering From His Life as Nat Turner," Winston-Salem (N.C.) Journal and Sentinel (2 April), p. C4.
    Interview and biographical sketch. Styron comments on his life in Connecticut, on his writing methods, and on Nat Turner.

46 _____. "Nat Turner: Slave to a Terrible Vision," Winston-Salem (N.C.) Journal and Sentinel (8 October), p. D6.
    Styron has told the story of Nat Turner "in such a way as to surely move people now and for many years to come to call the book a masterpiece."

47 _____. "A Revolt Revisited--Now Nat Turner As He Might Have Written It," Winston-Salem (N.C.) Journal and Sentinel (17 December), p. D6.
    Review of Daniel Panger's Ol' Prophet Nat which compares it to Nat Turner.

48 FADIMAN, CLIFTON. Review of The Confessions of Nat Turner, Book-of-the-Month Club News (October), pp. 2-5.

1967

"The central virtue of this novel is simply its extraordinary readability."

49   FANNING, GARTH. "Nat Turner's Revolt Haunts Us," Sacramento
     Bee (24 December), Valley Leisure Section, p. L17.
         In The Confessions of Nat Turner, "Styron seems to have
     produced one of the outstanding novels of the last few
     years."

50   FAVRE, GREGORY. "Can White Man Get Inside Skin of Black Man
     Turner?" Dayton Daily News (22 October), Dayton Leisure
     Magazine, p. 13.
         The Confessions of Nat Turner is "a courageous book, one
     that will be read, digested, discussed, cussed and praised.
     I stand with those who praise it."

51   FERGUSON, CHARLES A. "Styron Revises Story of Slave Revolt of
     1831," New Orleans Times-Picayune (29 October), p. 12.
         The Confessions of Nat Turner is "a trememdous assignment
     for a novelist. But Mr. Styron has succeeded, and in so
     doing, placed himself among the first rank of current Amer-
     ican writers."

52   FOURNIER, NORMAN. "Rise and Fall of a Slave," Portland (Me.)
     Telegram (8 October), p. 4D.
         The Confessions of Nat Turner is "a highly perceptive
     and imaginative fictional study."

53   FRANKLIN, JOHN HOPE. "A Meditation on History," Chicago Sun-
     Times Book Week (8 October), pp. 1, 11.
         The Confessions of Nat Turner is "a skillful and engros-
     sing book....Mr. Styron makes many salient comments and ob-
     servations that reveal his profound understanding of the
     institution of slavery."

54   FREMONT-SMITH, ELIOT. "Books of The Times--A Sword Is Sharp-
     ened," New York Times (3 October), p. 45.
         The Confessions of Nat Turner is "one of those rare
     books that show us our American past, our present--our-
     selves--in a dazzling shaft of light that cuts through the
     defenses of commonplace 'knowledge' to compel understanding."

55   _____. "Books of The Times-- 'The Confessions of Nat
     Turner'--II," New York Times (4 October), p. 45.
         The Confessions of Nat Turner is "a rich and powerful
     novel whose impact will be widely, and in my opinion, de-
     servingly felt."

56   FRIEDMAN, MELVIN J. "The Confessions of Nat Turner: The Con-
      vergence of 'Nonfiction Novel' and 'Meditation on History,'"
      Journal of Popular Culture, 1 (Fall), 166–75.
          Styron has "arrived." The influences of Proust and
      Camus on The Confessions of Nat Turner are detailed in a
      look at the complexity and success of Styron's first-person
      narration.
      Reprinted: 1968.B56; 1970.A1; 1974.A2.

57   FULLER, EDMUND. "Power and Eloquence in New Styron Novel,"
      Wall Street Journal (4 October), p. 16.
          In The Confessions of Nat Turner, Styron "has written
      the true American tragedy."

58   GARRETT, JAMES. "Styron Attempts Probe on Negro Character,"
      Cleveland Press (13 October), In Magazine, p. 17.
          The "difficulty" with The Confessions of Nat Turner "is
      that Styron has written us a sermon; it will be welcomed by
      many and applied to today, while others will find it stilt-
      ed, even sanctimonious."

59   GREEN, FLORENCE. "Styron Returns South," Houston Chronicle
      (1 October), Zest Magazine, p. 18.
          Descriptive favorable review of The Confessions of Nat
      Turner.

60   GREENE, A. C. "The Printed Page," Dallas Times Herald (15 Oc-
      tober), Sec. E, p. 13.
          "There are some things [in The Confessions of Nat Turner]
      that could be picked at by a critic--anachronisms, question-
      able use of words, a disturbing quality of language for Nat
      which begins as a handicap but ends up convincingly power-
      ful. But little question that this is a sorrowful master-
      piece."

61   GREENLEAF, RICHARD. "Timely as Ever," The Worker (27 August),
      p. 8.
          Review of Aptheker's "Nat Turner's Slave Rebellion"
      which notes Styron's refusal to acknowledge Aptheker's work
      in advance publicity for Nat Turner.

62   _____. "Styron's Anti-Negro Novel Is Libel on Nat Turner,"
      The Worker (8 October), p. 5.
          "To wrench history, and thus to pollute literature, as
      this book does, would have been a crime at any moment since
      those fateful days of 1831. But at this moment, backed by
      the amplifiers of modern publishing, it is a social crime

1967

comparable only to the new repressions being prepared in
the White House and the Pentagon."

63   GREENWOOD, WALTER B. "Nat Turner's Revolt a Tragic Comment on
     Slavery's Evils," Buffalo Evening News (14 October), p. 12-B.
        "Rarely has there been such a moving analysis of the
     psychology of slavery" as in The Confessions of Nat Turner.

64   GRIFFIN, LLOYD W. Review of The Confessions of Nat Turner,
     Library Journal, 92 (1 October), 3448-49.
        Styron's new novel "should be on the shelves of all col-
     lections of contemporary fiction."

65   GRIMES, ROY. "Books and Things," Victoria (Texas) Advocate
     (15 October), Fun Section, p. 10.
        The Confessions of Nat Turner is "an exceptional study
     in documentary fiction."

66   H., S. "Novel of Slave Revolt Eloquent," San Antonio Express
     (8 October), p. 3-H.
        Descriptive review of The Confessions of Nat Turner.

67   HALL, JOAN JOFFE. "Jehovah's Rebel Slave," Houston Post (22
     October), Spotlight Section, p. 12.
        "If Styron is like other American novelists in his ob-
     session with violence he may be alone among them in seeing
     violence as neither comic nor sociological nor absurd, but
     as tragic."

68   HARRIS, JUDITH. "Styron Ignores End of the Novel," Rome (Italy)
     Daily American (3 May), p. 4.
        Interview in which Styron discusses Nat Turner, the con-
     temporary novel, and Rome.

69   HARWI, ROBERT. "Styron Novel Presents Fiction at Highest Lev-
     el," Wichita Sunday Eagle and Beacon (3 December), p. 10C.
        The Confessions of Nat Turner "represents the art of
     fiction at its highest level."

70   HEISE, KENAN. Review of The Confessions of Nat Turner, Exten-
     sion, 62 (December), 54.
        "The brutality and bleakness of the plot is buoyed by
     the quick pace and story-telling ability of the author."

71   HERMAN, DICK. "Is Grim Message of Slavery Just Beginning To
     Be Felt?" Lincoln (Neb.) Sunday Journal and Star (15 Oc-
     tober), p. 15F.

"In a number of ways," The Confessions of Nat Turner "is
a strong book. Perhaps too strong in language and description for many. I found it a work of art."

72   HICKS, GRANVILLE. "Race Riot, 1831," Saturday Review, 50 (7
      October), 29-31.
           The Confessions of Nat Turner is not without faults; but
      "the virtues shine forth."

73   _____. "Five For Year's End," Saturday Review, 50 (30 Decem-
      ber), 19.
           The Confessions of Nat Turner is "close enough to suc-
      cess to make the novel one of the year's finest."

74   HICKS, WALTER J. "The Futile Insurrection," Baltimore Sunday
      Sun (15 October), p. 5-D.
           The Confessions of Nat Turner is "technically sound, fre-
      quently moving, and of such relevance to us, here, now as
      to be ominous."

75   HIGBY, JIM. "'Nat Turner' Chronicles Slave Revolt," Buffalo
      Courier Express (19 November), p. 87.
           The Confessions of Nat Turner is "one of the most inter-
      esting and believable historical novels of this or any
      year."

76   HOFFMAN, FREDERICK J. "William Styron: The Metaphysical
      Hurt," in his The Art of Southern Fiction: A Study of Some
      Modern Novelists. Carbondale: Southern Illinois Universi-
      ty Press, pp. 144-61.
           This is an English version of Hoffman's essay in the
      Friedman and Nigro Configuration, 1967.A1. It is a discus-
      sion of Styron's first three novels in light of "the pro-
      blem of believing, the desperate necessity for having the
      courage to be." Some attention is also given to this same
      theme in Styron's non-fiction.
      Reprinted: 1968.B77.

77   HOGAN, WILLIAM. "William Styron's American Tragedy," San
      Francisco Chronicle (9 October), p. 43.
           The Confessions of Nat Turner is "a distressing book, but
      a successful and moving psychological novel with great social
      overtones."

78   _____. "Further Thoughts on the Styron Novel," San Francisco
      Chronicle (10 October), p. 39.
           "With all my respect for the book I find flaws in it."

1967

79 HOYT, CHARLES ALVA. "Summation of Slavery," Louisville <u>Couri-</u>
   <u>er-Journal & Times</u> (15 October), p. E 5.
   In <u>The Confessions of Nat Turner</u>, "Styron has taken upon
   himself, in his artist's sublime egoism, the task of a whole
   generation of sociologists, encyclopedians and research-
   fellows, and done it incomparably better, as the artist always does."

80 HOYT, ELIZABETH N. "Story of Negro Uprising in 1831," Cedar
   Rapids (Iowa) <u>Gazette</u> (8 October), pp. 2C, 23C.
   <u>The Confessions of Nat Turner</u> is "the finest novel I
   have read in many years."

81 HURT, RICHARD L. "Slavery's Quiet Resistance," Boston <u>Sunday</u>
   <u>Globe</u> (8 October), p. 43-A.
   <u>The Confessions of Nat Turner</u> is "first-rate imaginative
   narrative literature," but whether Sytron "has captured the
   real Nat Turner, or even meant to, is questionable."

82 INGLE, H. L. "Meditation on History," Chattanooga <u>Times</u> (12
   November), p. 30.
   <u>The Confessions of Nat Turner</u> "will cause the reader--
   and there should be many--to view America's racial problems,
   and black power in a new light."

83 KAUFFMANN, STANLEY. "Styron's Unwritten Novel," <u>Hudson Review</u>,
   20 (Winter), 675-79.
   "Nat's drama, quintessentially, is a soul's pilgrimage
   to a clearer perception that God is or is not; or else it
   is merely the bursting of one abcess in a large, poisoned
   body. Styron had ambitions towards the former. In falling
   short, he has not even given us the reality of the latter."

84 KAZIN, ALFRED. "Instinct for Tragedy: A Message in Black and
   White," <u>Book World</u> (Chicago <u>Tribune</u>, Washington <u>Post</u>) (8
   October), pp. 1, 22.
   <u>The Confessions of Nat Turner</u> is "a wonderfully evocative
   portrait of a gifted, proud, long-suppressed human being who
   began to live only when he was sentenced to die."

85 KEOWN, DON. "The Book Pages--Two New and Different Novels By
   Veterans Styron and Uris," San Rafael (Calif.) <u>Independent-</u>
   <u>Journal</u> (7 October), p. M 15.
   <u>The Confessions of Nat Turner</u>, "powerful without the hys-
   terical shrillness of some of our other present-day novelists, makes the point better than any history text."

86   KINCAID, ANNE. Review of The Confessions of Nat Turner, Li-
         brary Journal, 92 (15 November), 4274.
            The Confessions of Nat Turner is a "beautifully written
         and thought-provoking book."

87   KIRSCH, ROBERT. "The Virginia Slave Revolt," Los Angeles
         Times (8 October), Calendar Section, p. 36. This syndicat-
         ed review also appeared in Tulsa World (15 October); Durham
         (N.C.) Morning Herald (5 November).
            The Confessions of Nat Turner is "a stirring work, a tri-
         umph of the fictive imagination. I believe it will endure
         as one of the great novels by an American author in this
         century."

88   KOHLER, ROY. "Bloody Page in History--Controversial Slave Re-
         volt Recalled," Pittsburgh Press (8 October), Sec. 6, p. 6.
            In The Confessions of Nat Turner, Styron "has done an
         artist's job and his product, however controversial, may
         help many a reader to better understand some of the complex-
         ities of race relations today."

89   KUEHL, JOHN. "Appendix," in his Write and Rewrite--A Study of
         the Creative Process. New York: Meredith Press, pp. 294-
         308. This book was simultaneously published in paperback
         under the title Creative Writing & Rewriting by Appleton-
         Century-Crofts.
            Facsimile of Styron's holograph manuscript and the pub-
         lished version of Chapter I of The Long March are reproduced.

90   LaHAYE, JUDSON. Review of The Confessions of Nat Turner, Best
         Sellers, 27 (1 November), 308.
            Styron's new novel "has an opalescent quality that out-
         shines both the historical facts on which it is based and
         the quasi-parallelism of today's Negro Revolution."

91   LANE, JACK C. "Three Days of 'Indiscriminate Massacre,'"
         Orlando (Fla.) Sentinel (5 November), Florida Magazine, p.
         16-F.
            "Styron's development of Nat Turner's character is the
         work of a skilled writer;...Perhaps more significantly,
         Styron has given us one of the most profound treatments
         of...slavery that we are likely to see in fictional or his-
         torical writing."

92   LAYTON, MIKE. "A Negro Slave Revolt and What It Tells Us,"
         Olympia (Wash.) Sunday Olympian (28 October), p. 27.
            In The Confessions of Nat Turner, Styron, "who established

1967

himself as a first-rate novelist in his earlier works, has surpassed himself."

93   LEWIS, CLAUDE. "Slavery, Murder, and God," Philadelphia <u>Sunday Bulletin</u> (15 October), Books and Art Section, p. 3.
        <u>The Confessions of Nat Turner</u> is "one of the best books to come forth in recent years on a subject that Americans know too little of."

94   LEWIS, R. W. B. "A Yale Bookshelf--Topic: Fiction 1967," <u>Yale Alumni Magazine</u>, 31 (November), 9.
        "It is impossible to tell, with our faces virtually touching its pages, whether <u>The Confessions of Nat Turner</u> is a great work. But it is obviously a very good one, a brave book, something to read and re-read and ruminate on--and worry about."

95   _____, and C. VANN WOODWARD. "Slavery in the First Person," <u>Yale Alumni Magazine</u>, 31 (November), 33-39.
        Interview in which Styron defends the psychological truth of Nat Turner's sexual passion, discusses Old Testament parallels in the novel, Nat's motivation, and the book as an inadvertent comment on the contemporary civil rights debate.
        Reprinted: 1970.A1.

96   LIVINGSTON, JEAN. "Three Days That Shook a Small World," Quincy (Mass.) <u>Patriot-Ledger</u> (1 November), p. 44.
        Descriptive review of <u>The Confessions of Nat Turner</u>.

97   LONG, JAMES. Review of <u>The Confessions of Nat Turner</u>, <u>Oregon Journal</u> (Portland) (11 November), p. 6J.
        This novel "is so moving, so real, and so horrifyingly in the present that it must be classified as more than just a novel. It is one of the most important publishing events of the 1960s."

98   LYNCH, DONNA. "<u>Confessions of Nat Turner</u>--Doubts This Novel Worth the Praise It Has Received," Baton Rouge <u>Advocate</u> (29 October), Sec. E, p. 2.
        "I think this book is good, but not great. And I can only feel anger that once again a writer has let the scum of the South represent all of the citizens of the South."

99   McCORMICK, JAY. "An American Tragedy--Lessons That the Gallows Failed to Teach," Detroit <u>News</u> (8 October), p. 3-E.
        <u>The Confessions of Nat Turner</u> is "very definitely a great book of these times--and it will last long beyond them."

100 McGROARTY, JOSEPH G. "'Nat Turner': A Racial Tract For Our
   Times?" The Tablet (Brooklyn, N.Y.) (16 November), p. 13.
      If The Confessions of Nat Turner "is to be faulted on
   any one count, it must be on the grounds of a gross and unnecessary realism that is hard to condone even under fairly
   liberal standards of judgment. It is the one foul-tasting
   worm in an otherwise excellent and commendable apple."

101 McMILLAN, DOUGALD. "Come In, Mr. Styron. Sit Down, Mr. Styron.
   No, Mr. Styron, 'Nat Turner' Is Not a Great Book. Rather,
   Mr. Styron, It Is Bad, Bad," North Carolina Anvil (Durham)
   (9 December), p. 5.
      "The tedium of 424 pages of 'fine' writing that doesn't
   come off is not the stuff great novels are made of."

102 MASON, ROBERT. "A Brilliant 'Meditation on History'--Nat
   Turner, From Birth to Rebellion," Norfolk Virginian-Pilot
   and Portsmouth Star (8 October), p. 6-C.
      In The Confessions of Nat Turner, Styron, "upon coming
   home again to the country of his roots and fiber, and ex-
   plaining its bitterest lore, has produced great art."

103 MENN, THORPE. "Books of the Day," Kansas City Star (8 October),
   p. 6E.
      In The Confessions of Nat Turner, "most remarkable is
   Styron's presenting a study in hatred that does not inspire
   his readers to hate."

104 MERAS, PHYLLIS. "The Author," Saturday Review, 50 (7 October),
   30.
      Short interview with Styron which focuses on Nat Turner.

105 MEYER, JUNE. "Spokesman For the Blacks," The Nation, 205 (4
   December), 597-99 [597].
      Calls Nat Turner a "stunt" which is part of the "fantas-
   tic black-to-white 'dialog' miscarried by white-controlled
   media through the 'medium' of the now professional, white
   intermediary."

106 MILLER, WILLIAM LEE. "The Meditations of William Styron," The
   Reporter, 37 (16 November), 42, 44, 46, 49.
      In The Confessions of Nat Turner, "Styron got himself
   into doing two or maybe three things simultaneously, and
   they work against each other: a novel, an essay on slavery,
   perhaps also an interpretation of modern race relations."

107 MOLINEUX, WILL. "Newport News-Born William Styron Covers Tragic
   1831 Slave Revolt," Newport News-Hampton (Va.) Daily Press

1967

(29 October), <u>New Dominion</u> Magazine, p. 10.
"It is too bad that Styron has focused his considerable
writing talent on such a subject because he has helped vault
Nat Turner from villain to hero."

108   MOODY, MINNIE HITE. "Documentary Novel Is Pegged to 1831 Revolt," Columbus (Ohio) <u>Sunday Dispatch</u> (22 October), <u>Tab</u>
Section, p. 14.
"I am not sure that this book is truly a novel--documen-
tary is more accurate--and it is seriously flawed by...
anachronisms"; but Styron "has written a book which in many
ways is so close to perfect!"

109   MORRIS, WILLIE. "The Bear on Madison Avenue: A Provincial in
New York, Part II," <u>Harper's Magazine</u>, 235 (July), 60-68
[67-68].
Brief description of Styron's passage from a "lowly po-
sition" in a New York publishing house to his present status
as a best-selling author. Also described is the experience
Morris, Styron, and C. Vann Woodward had being interviewed
on the South by several New York radio stations.
Reprinted: 1967.B110.

110   _____. <u>North Toward Home</u>. Boston: Houghton Mifflin, pp.
396-400.
Material reprinted from Morris' <u>Harper's</u> piece,
1967.B109.

111   MOYANO, MARIA CLARA. "Speaking Volumes--The Confessions of
William Styron," <u>Book World</u> (Chicago <u>Tribune</u>, Washington
<u>Post</u>) (1 October), p. 6.
Interview in which Styron talks about his research for
<u>Nat Turner</u>, possible Negro reactions to the book, and con-
temporary parallels.

112   MURRAY, ALBERT. "A Troublesome Property," <u>New Leader</u>, 10 (4
December), 18-21.
In <u>The Confessions of Nat Turner</u>, Styron's conception of
Nat "seems to have been restricted by underlying socio-po-
litical assumptions."
Reprinted: 1971.A2.

113   MURRELL, HELEN. "Turner Confesses While Waiting Hangman's
Noose," Abilene (Texas) <u>Reporter-News</u> (3 December), p. 13-C.
Descriptive favorable review of <u>The Confessions of Nat
Turner</u>.

114   MYERS, ARTHUR. "He Speaks For His Own," Hartford <u>Courant</u> (12
      November), Magazine, p. 13.
          With <u>The Confessions of Nat Turner</u>, although one "finds
      oneself wondering if this is skillful journalism, clever
      literary opportunism," it is nonetheless "a fine book, writ-
      ten with imagination, insight, and intense compassion."

115   NIGRO, AUGUST. "<u>The Long March</u>: The Expansive Hero In a
      Closed World," <u>Critique</u> (Minneapolis), 9 (No. 3), 103-12.
          Styron's indictment of military life becomes a more gen-
      eral indictment of American life. The American experience
      in turn is reinforced by and transformed into more universal
      significance through allusion to the rebel tradition in the
      literature and mythology of western civilization.

116   NOLTE, WILLIAM H. "Fact Novel of Revolt in Hot Summer of
      1831," St. Louis <u>Sunday Post-Dispatch</u> (8 October), p. 4-D.
      This review also appeared in Columbia (S.C.) <u>State & Rec-
      ord</u> (22 October).
          In <u>The Confessions of Nat Turner</u>, "the prose pulsates
      with rhythms pleasing to both eye and ear," but Styron
      "sometimes overwrites."

117   O'CONNELL, SHAUN. "Styron's Nat Turner...," <u>The Nation</u>, 205
      (16 October), 373-74.
          Styron's portrait is believable; and the author demon-
      strates that Nat is "in every way sympathetic and right"
      in his vengeance.

118   OSBORNE, LORRAINE. "Styron Pens Powerful Novel Around Story
      of Slave Revolt," Bridgeport <u>Sunday Post</u> (22 October), p.
      E-4.
          <u>The Confessions of Nat Turner</u> is "a novel of staggering
      beauty and power."

119   PARKER, ROY, JR. "Styron's 'Nat Turner'--Fact Transmuted Into
      Art," Raleigh <u>News and Observer</u> (29 October), Sec. 3, p. 3.
          In <u>The Confessions of Nat Turner</u>, "it is the theme, and
      the felicity with which he holds to it, that makes this
      book a solid achievement of Styron's already solid genius
      and mitigates its flaws."

120   PATTERSON, ANN. "Rebellion of a Slave," <u>Arizona Republic</u>
      (Phoenix) (29 October), p. N-9.
          <u>The Confessions of Nat Turner</u> "is a good story at its
      best, even if it hadn't been based on historical fact. But
      with the added implications of truth it makes reading of
      the highest quality."

1967

121 PATTESON, RICHARD. "A Glimmer of Compassion, Humility and
    Pride," Charleston (W.Va.) Sunday Gazette-Mail (17 Decem-
    ber), p. 19m.
       With The Confessions of Nat Turner, Styron "has surpassed
    himself"; his "most compelling talent" is "his ability to
    see in men that glimmer of compassion, humility, and pride
    that makes a man's life worthwhile."

122 PENNE, LEO. "Out From the Vicious Circle," Seattle Post-Intel-
    ligencer (22 October), Northwest Today Section, p. 4.
       In The Confessions of Nat Turner, "the characters live
    and Nat is a man."

123 PHILLIPS, JOHN. "Styron Unlocked," Vogue, 150 (December),
    216-17, 267-71, 278.
       Affectionate portrait of and interview with Styron which
    includes summary of reception of Nat Turner.

124 PLIMPTON, GEORGE. "William Styron: A Shared Ideal," New York
    Times Book Review (8 October), pp. 2, 3, 30, 32, 34.
       Interview in which Styron talks of the beginnings of Nat
    Turner, his research, his views on slavery, Nat as a typi-
    cal revolutionary and as a thinker, the character of Marga-
    ret Whitehead, and of religion in Nat Turner.
    Reprinted: 1970.A1.

125 POWERS, JAMES. "Book Reviews," Hollywood (Calif.) Reporter
    (29 September), p. 6.
       The Confessions of Nat Turner is, "on any level, a thor-
    oughly engrossing book and a brilliant evocation of a his-
    torical figure."

126 Q[UILL], G[YNTER]. "Revolt of Negro Slaves Echoes Over the
    Years," Waco (Texas) Tribune-Herald (5 November), p. 13-D.
       In The Confessions of Nat Turner, Styron "has...written
    one of the most compelling books you will read, an impres-
    sive, moving work of fiction founded on fact...."

127 RAGAN, SAM. "Southern Accent," Raleigh News and Observer (29
    October), Sec. 3, p. 3.
       Brief mention that Nat Turner "seems assured of being
    the novel of the year."

128 RAHV, PHILIP. "Through the Midst of Jerusalem," New York Re-
    view of Books, 9 (26 October), 6, 8, 10.
       The Confessions of Nat Turner "is a first-rate novel,
    the best that William Styron has written and the best by an

American writer that has appeared in some years."
Reprinted: 1971.A2.

129   RAYMOND, ROBERT. "Fine Novel Describes Early U.S. Slave Re-
       volt," Staten Island (N.Y.) Advance (22 October), p. B-6.
          The Confessions of Nat Turner is "an eloquent story well
       told."

130   REDDING, SAUNDERS. "A Fateful Lightning In the Southern Sky,"
       Providence Sunday Journal (29 October), p. 18-W.
          The Confessions of Nat Turner is a "fine, artistic
       achievement" which, like "all good novels," serves "a social
       function too."

131   REWALD, ALICE. "Deux Entretiens: William Styron," La
       Quinzaine littéraire (Paris) (15-31 October), pp. 12-13.
          Interview in which Styron talks about Nat Turner, cre-
       ative writing, and racial problems in America.

132   RICHARDSON, D. E. "Telling All," Shenandoah, 19 (Autumn), 84-
       87.
          "Despite Mr. Styron's powers as a novelist (and they are
       considerable), The Confessions of Nat Turner is a fright-
       ening failure." It indicates "how difficult even now it is
       for a white man to write a story from the point of view of
       a black man."

133   RICHTER, DAVID H. Review of The Confessions of Nat Turner,
       Chicago Literary Review, 5 (October), 1, 10-11.
          "Perhaps it is the final irony that Styron, in an effort
       to make his tale relevant to our time, included matter
       which masks its ultimate relevance--and that the book suf-
       fers, not from being too historical, but from not being
       historical enough."

134   ROBERTSON, DON. "'Nat Turner': One View: Styron Is a Brave
       Failure," Cleveland Plain Dealer (15 October), p. 8-H.
          In The Confessions of Nat Turner, "we are too aware of
       Styron. We are not aware enough of the people involved."

135   ROBINSON, CHARLES K. "Book Review--'Confessions of Nat
       Turner,'" The Setonian (Seton Hall University, South Orange,
       N.J.), 42 (22 November), 6.
          "With his latest work,...Mr. Styron need never write an-
       other word to be considered one of the finest writers of
       the Twentieth Century."

1967

136   R[OSEBURY], C[ELIA]. "Interview--Aptheker on Styron's Nat
      Turner: From Rebel Slave to Racist Monster," People's World
      (San Francisco) (4 November), p. 7.
          Review which is more of a summary of Aptheker's criti-
      cisms of Nat Turner for its inaccuracies and distortions of
      history.

137   ROTHCHILD, SYLVIA. "The Bookshelf," Jewish Advocate (Boston)
      (21 December), Sec. 2, p. 16.
          The Confessions of Nat Turner has in common with Malamud's
      The Fixer "the mythologizing of real events and a sense that
      these events are of great contemporary significance."
      Styron's novel is "well-written, carefully planned and struc-
      tured."

138   RUBIN, LOUIS D., JR. The Curious Death of the Novel: Essays
      in American Literature. Baton Rouge: Louisiana State Uni-
      versity Press, pp. 4, 9, 10, 20-22, 146-47, 277, 280, 286,
      292.
          Scattered mentions of Styron in a general treatment of
      the state of the novel, especially in light of the history
      and problems of Southern writers. Some of the material is
      reprinted from Rubin's Journal of Southern History essay,
      1963.B23.

139   ____. "Books--Eloquent Story of a Slave Rebellion," Washing-
      ton (D.C.) Sunday Star (8 October), p. 14-G.
          "Beyond a doubt," The Confessions of Nat Turner "is the
      best Southern novel to appear since, well Set This House on
      Fire. It can hold its own with Faulkner, Warren and the
      others, and it will be read, I suspect, for many years to
      come."

140   ____. "William Styron and Human Bondage: The Confessions of
      Nat Turner," Hollins Critic, 4 (December), 1-12.
          Examines Set This House on Fire and its critical recep-
      tion as a background for a study of theme and technique in
      Nat Turner. Focus is on Styron's use of first-person
      narration.
      Reprinted: 1970.A1; 1971.B30.

141   S., D. L. "The New Books," Seattle Argus (27 October), p. 8.
          In The Confessions of Nat Turner, "Styron has written a
      great work. More than a novel, it is part and parcel of
      our history, and a study of a problem yet unsolved. This
      is truly the book of the year."

142   SASS, SAMUEL. "Book Review--The Tragic Story of a Suicidal
          Negro Revolt," Berkshire Eagle (Pittsfield, Mass.) (18 No-
          vember), p. 14.
             Descriptive review of The Confessions of Nat Turner.

143   SCHAAP, DICK. "Interview With William Styron," Chicago Sun-
          Times Book Week (8 October), pp. 2, 11. This article also
          appeared in San Francisco Examiner and Chronicle (15
          October).
             Styron discusses the technical and historical aspects of
          Nat Turner.

144   SCHLESINGER, ARTHUR, JR. Review of The Confessions of Nat
          Turner, Vogue, 150 (1 October), 143.
             Styron shows "an extraordinary perception of the subtle
          human admixture of strength and compassion, hate, and self-
          hatred."

145   SCHROTH, RAYMOND A. "Nat Turner's Sword," America, 117 (14
          October), 416.
             "By so blending the blackness of evil and the beauty of
          blackness in one man, Styron leaves the reader pondering
          not the evil but the man; and he calls the devil to be ex-
          orcized by its name."

146   SCHWARTZ, JOSEPH. "Negro Revolt of 1831 Flares Again in a
          'Big' Novel of Fall," Milwaukee Journal (8 October), Sec.
          5, p. 4.
             "Styron has captured the tangled consciousness of Nat
          Turner with great skill, despite major faults in technique."

147   SHEED, WILFRID. "The Slave Who Became a Man," New York Times
          Book Review (8 October), pp. 1-3, 30, 32, 34.
             Although there is "an artificiality to the whole enter-
          prise," The Confessions of Nat Turner "does succeed in many
          places as a kind of historical tone poem." It must also be
          considered as "part politics."
             Reprinted: 1970.A1; 1971.B31.

148   SHERMAN, JOHN K. "Portrays Negro View--Novel Illuminates His-
          tory," Minneapolis Star (10 October), p. 4E.
             "The late William Faulkner's niche as leading Southern
          writer has been filled by William Styron with this powerful,
          imaginative and moving novel."

149   SMILEY, NIXON. "Slave's History Retold--Novel Sheds Under-
          standing," Miami Herald (8 October), p. 7-F.
             "Styron has done a superb job of recreating Turner, as

1967

well as the other characters who play important roles. The
novel, however, is unconventional and the reader used to
being told who, where, what and how in every other paragraph
might easily become confused."

150   SMITH, MILES A. "Slave Revolt of 1831 Is Recounted," Indianapolis News (21 October), p. 30. This syndicated review also
appeared in St. Louis Globe Democrat (21 October); Neodesha
(Kan.) Daily Sun (13 October); Sacramento Union (22 October).
The Confessions of Nat Turner is "an eloquent story, com-
pellingly told."

151   SOKOLOV, RAYMOND A. "Into the Mind of Nat Turner," Newsweek,
70 (16 October), 65-69.
Appreciation of Nat Turner, Styron's thoughts about the
book, comments by and about James Baldwin, and a detailed
biographical sketch of Styron.
Reprinted: 1970.A1.

152   SPEARMAN, WALTER. "'Confessions of Nat Turner' Is Important
Book--A Vivid Account of Revolt and Slaughter," Chapel Hill
(N.C.) Weekly (15 October), p. 4.
The Confessions of Nat Turner "will be the talked-about
book of this year--partly because it actually is a book
worth talking about as well as reading, partly because it
is such a pertinent book that it must be talked about."

153   STALDER, MARJORIE BRIGHT. "Books," Hemet (Calif.) News (7 October), Sec. 2, p. 2.
The Confessions of Nat Turner is "one of the most important American novels in several years"; Styron's prose is
"straightforward, restrained and touching."

154   STEINER, GEORGE. "Books--The Fire Last Time," New Yorker, 43
(25 November), 236, 238, 241-42, 244.
Styron "has every artistic right to make his Nat Turner
less an anatomy of the Negro mind than a fiction of complex
relationship, of the relationship between a present-day
white man of deep Southern roots and the Negro in today's
whirlwind."

155   SUDLER, BARBARA. "Nat Turner Led Revolt to Bring Purpose to
Slaves' Lives," Denver Sunday Post (15 October), Roundup
Section, p. 12.
In The Confessions of Nat Turner, "the audacious point
of view, first person black, as well as thorough research
that develops characters of both colors, and sensitive

insight combined with a superbly mellifluous style make the
book forceful and compelling."

156   THOMAS, SIDNEY. "Slave Broke His Chains," Atlanta Journal and
       Constitution (12 November), p. 10-D.
            The Confessions of Nat Turner "is a magnificent promise
       of becoming a landmark, not only as a truly successful Amer-
       ican novel, but as a moving and heartfelt plea for the rights
       of man."

157   THOMPSON, JOHN. "Rise and Slay!" Commentary, 44 (November),
       81-85.
            In The Confessions of Nat Turner, Styron combines "the
       old art of storytelling with the instruction of modern psy-
       chology"; the novel has a "complex and rewarding structure."

158   TUCKER, MARTIN. Review of The Confessions of Nat Turner, Com-
       monweal, 87 (22 December), 388-89.
            "Certainly compassion and beauty of style and structure
       fill every page in this carefully-wrought story, but is
       compassion enough?"

159   TURNEY, CHARLES. "Virginian's Novel Seeks 'Meditation on His-
       tory,'" Richmond (Va.) Times-Dispatch (15 October), p. 5-F.
            The Confessions of Nat Turner is "a keenly imagined and
       skillfully wrought book by one of our most important novel-
       ists."

160   W., B. "The Negro Fury: A Vital Insight," Long Beach (Calif.)
       Independent Press-Telegram (18 November), p. A-6.
            The Confessions of Nat Turner is "both a commentary on
       today as well as a historical fictionalization. Either way
       it is a fascinating and important book by an excellent
       author."

161   WADE, GERALD. "'The Only Effective U.S. Negro Revolt,'" Omaha
       Sunday World-Herald (29 October), Magazine, p. 36.
            Descriptive review of The Confessions of Nat Turner.

162   WALSH, ANNE C. "William Styron Writes 'Autobiography' of First
       Slave Uprising Leader," Phoenix Gazette (18 October), p. 17.
            The Confessions of Nat Turner "is a writing event which
       speaks well for the American capacity to feel...."

163   WARREN, ROBERT PENN. "William Styron," Book-of-the-Month Club
       News (October), pp. 6-7, 14.

1967

> Biographical sketch which includes psychological glimpses
> of Styron, a look at his working habits, and a description
> of his lifestyle.

164   WEBER, R.B. "Styron's Power Creates a Real Being," Louisville
        Times (13 October), p. 11A.
>   In The Confessions of Nat Turner, Styron "presents with
> great subtlety and strength a real man walking through his
> pages."

165   WECHSLER, JAMES A. "A Lonely Anger," New York Post (17 Octo-
        ber), p. 49.
>   Appreciation of Nat Turner. "It is at once a convincing
> case against blind, mindless insurrection and an incitement
> to riot, not only for the outcast slumdweller but for the
> middle-class Negro who knows in how many places the 'For
> Whites Only' sign, even discreetly hidden, still prevails."

166   WEEKS, EDWARD. "The Peripatetic Reviewer," Atlantic Monthly,
        220 (November), 130, 132.
>   The Confessions of Nat Turner is "a work of power, of
> loving and hateful descriptions, of little mirth, and for
> the most part, of persuasive psychology."

167   WELLEJUS, ED. "The Bookshelf," Erie (Penna.) Times-News (29
        October), p. 11-F.
>   The Confessions of Nat Turner is "a major book, one that
> might possibly be read years, even decades, from now."

168   WHITE, POPPY CANNON. "Poppy's Notes--'Confessions of Nat
        Turner,'" New York Amsterdam News (25 November), p. 15.
>   Styron's artistry in The Confessions of Nat Turner is
> praiseworthy; but Nat himself "is a madman. It is impos-
> sible to identify with him, or to understand the tortured
> workings of a mind that is often poetic and sensitive but
> psychotic."

169   _____. "Poppy's Notes--'The African' Vs. Nat Turner," New
        York Amsterdam News (9 December), p. 17.
>   Defense of her contention, made in her review of Nat
> Turner, 1967.B168, that Nat Turner's was not the most ef-
> fective American slave revolt; and a comparison of Nat
> Turner with Harold Courlander's novel The African.

170   WHITMAN, ALDEN. "William Styron Examines the Negro Upheaval,"
        New York Times (5 August), p. 13.
>   Article-interview in which Styron parallels contemporary

civil rights agitation with Nat Turner's rebellion and calls his forthcoming novel "a lens on the future." For a correction to this article, <u>see</u> 1967.B4.

171 WILLIAMS, ERNEST E. "Novel on Slave Uprising Skillful," Fort Wayne <u>News-Sentinel</u> (28 October), p. 4A.
In <u>The Confessions of Nat Turner</u>, Styron "has written a good book, one which should become [an] increasingly important book for our time."

172 WILSON, GERTRUDE. "White on White—Confessions of a Believer," New York <u>Amsterdam News</u> (21 October), p. 17.
Passing reference to and praise for <u>Nat Turner</u>: "Styron is a white man who has written about [Nat Turner's rebellion] out of the inside of his mind" and has "done a good job of it."

173 WINFREY, LEE. "Mr. Styron's Superb Novel—When a Negro Slave Rebelled," Detroit <u>Free Press</u> (8 October), p. 5-B.
<u>The Confessions of Nat Turner</u> "is a virtuoso's performance, and probably no better novel will be published in the United States this year."

174 WOLFF, GEOFFREY. "Slavery Intersects Present," Washington <u>Post</u> (24 October), p. A16.
<u>The Confessions of Nat Turner</u> "quickens the ghosts, articulates the whispers, gives flesh to the shadows of America's most resonant and guilt-heavy historical burden: the buying and selling of human life."

175 WOODWARD, C. VANN. "Confessions of a Rebel: 1831," <u>New Republic</u>, 157 (7 October), 25-28.
"It is doubtful...if the rare combination of talents essential to this formidable undertaking, a flawless command of dialect, a native instinct for the subtleties and ambivalences of race in the South, and a profound and unerring sense of place—Styron's native place as it was Nat Turner's—could well have been found anywhere else." Reprinted: 1971.A2.

176 WRIGHT, GILES E. "Life of Real Slave Treated in Top Novel," Los Angeles <u>Herald Examiner</u> (8 October), p. 4-J.
<u>The Confessions of Nat Turner</u> is "worth-while reading."

177 YARDLEY, JONATHAN. "Mr. Styron's Monumental 'Meditation on History,'" Greensboro (N.C.) <u>Daily News</u> (8 October), p. D3.
In <u>The Confessions of Nat Turner</u>, Styron "may have been not quite successful, but he has made a gigantic effort.

1968

And weighed against his triumphs, this failure is relatively
minor. He has given us a profound vision of the slave sys-
tem. He has written a novel which, in the mood of bleakness
and terror it portrays, approaches the best of Conrad. And
he has created a character, Nat Turner, whose place in our
literature will be very large."

1968 A BOOKS

1   CLARKE, JOHN HENRIK, ed. William Styron's Nat Turner--Ten
     Black Writers Respond. Boston: Beacon Press, 120 pp.
     Contents include:
     John Henrik Clarke. "Introduction," pp. vii-x.
     Lerone Bennett, Jr. "Nat's Last White Man," pp. 3-16.
         Styron's work dramatizes "how white Americans use black
     Americans no matter what we do." For a reprinting of this
     essay, see 1968.B27.
     Alvin F. Poussaint, M.D. "The Confessions of Nat Turner
     and the Dilemma of William Styron," pp. 17-22.
         Expresses belief that Styron unwittingly emasculates
     and degrades Nat and his people.
     Vincent Harding. "You've Taken My Nat and Gone," pp. 23-
     33.
         The blackness, the religious fervor, and the power of
     the historical Nat Turner are not comprehended by Styron.
     John Oliver Killens. "The Confessions of Willie Styron,"
     pp. 34-44.
         The Confessions of Nat Turner reveals more about the
     psyche of the "southern liberal" Styron than about that
     of the revolutionary Nat Turner.
     John A. Williams. "The Manipulation of History and of Fact:
     An Ex-Southerner's Apologist Tract For Slavery and the
     Life of Nat Turner; or, William Styron's Faked Confes-
     sions," pp. 45-49.
         Doubts that Styron's novel, "even in intent," was
     honest.
     Ernest Kaiser. "The Failure of William Styron," pp. 50-65.
         A documented attack on Styron's understanding of the
     Negro problem which decries "the absurdity of the separa-
     tion of art and politics, art and sociology." For a re-
     printing of this essay, see 1970.A1.
     Loyle Hairston. "William Styron's Nat Turner--Rogue-Nig-
     ger," pp. 66-72.
         Styron is guilty of "reading human history in fundamen-
     talist terms, within the narrow confines of regional loy-
     alty to the so-called southern tradition; a euphemism for
     institutional white supremacy...."

Charles V. Hamilton. "Our Nat Turner and William Styron's Creation," pp. 73-78.
   This is a slightly revised version of Hamilton's Saturday Review essay, 1968.B70.
Mike Thelwell. "Back With the Wind: Mr. Styron and Reverend Turner," pp. 79-91.
   Reprinting of portion of Thelwell's Massachusetts Review essay, 1968.B116.

2   FOSSUM, ROBERT H. William Styron--A Critical Essay. Contemporary Writers in Christian Perspective. Grand Rapids, Mich.: William B. Eerdmans, 48 pp.
   Readings of Styron's four novels focusing on his responses in fiction to the "absence of God." Styron's protagonists are rebels in an essentially "metaphysical struggle to affirm meaning in a world that denies it."

3   HILZIM, WILLIAM H. "Major Motifs in William Styron's Lie Down in Darkness: Music, the Clock, the Birds, Vegetation."
   Master's thesis, Louisiana State University in New Orleans.

1968 B SHORTER WRITINGS

1   ANCRUM, CALHOUN. "This Week's Reading--Novella Reflects Genius of Styron," Charleston (S.C.) News and Courier (7 April), p. 12-C.
   In The Long March, there is "writing of a first-rate literary artist still in a nascent stage, but already thoroughly competent. The canvas is smaller and the work less ambitious, but the evidence of fine writing all is there."

2   ANDERS, SMILEY. "Some of Early Power of Top Writer Shown," Baton Rouge Advocate (5 May), Sec. F, p. 2.
   The Long March is "a simple story, simply told."

3   ANON. Review of The Confessions of Nat Turner, Virginia Quarterly Review, 44 (Winter), viii.
   The novel is "a dynamic tale of throbbing immediacy, told by a craftsman who knows his business from first word to last."

4   ANON. "Nat Turner," Marquette (Mich.) Mining Journal (18 January), p. 12.
   Styron "has been eminently successful in his reconstruction" of "a man and his era."

1968

5   ANON. "Nat Turner Saga to Be Filmed," Cleveland <u>Plain Dealer</u>
     (18 February), p. 5-G.
          David Wolper has purchased the screen rights to Styron's
     novel.

6   ANON. Review of <u>The Confessions of Nat Turner</u>, <u>America</u>, 118
     (24 February), 269.
          The novel's great value is that "it makes us agonize over
     what the institution did to both black and white."

7   ANON. Review of <u>The Confessions of Nat Turner</u>, <u>Choice</u>, 5
     (March), 54.
          To students of literature and history, Styron's method
     should prove "emotionally evocative and his interpretation
     of the old South intellectually challenging."

8   ANON. "Short Reviews," London <u>Sun</u> (2 May), p. 8.
          <u>The Confessions of Nat Turner</u> is a "very, very well told
     story."

9   ANON. "Biographical Sketches of Persons Selected for the
     Pulitzer Prizes for 1968," New York <u>Times</u> (7 May), p. 34.
          Brief biographical sketch of Styron.

10   ANON. "Styron Feels 'Establishment,'" Waterbury (Conn.) <u>Re-</u>
     <u>publican</u> (7 May), pp. 1, 2.
          Syndicated (UPI) interview with Styron on occasion of
     his winning the Pulitzer Prize for <u>Nat Turner</u>. He comments
     on his reactions to the award, on the critical reception of
     <u>Nat Turner</u>, and on his support of Eugene McCarthy for the
     Democratic presidential nomination.

11   ANON. "A Pulitzer For Mr. Styron," Newport News (Va.) <u>Daily</u>
     <u>Press</u> (8 May), p. 4.
          Editorial hailing awarding of Prize to Styron and prais-
     ing him as "one of the most brilliant writers of our time."

12   ANON. "Unslavish Fidelity: The Confessions of William
     Styron," <u>Times Literary Supplement</u> (London) (9 May), p. 480.
          "This combination of Old Testament prophet and Southern
     white puritan isn't the Nat Turner who has so sturdily re-
     sisted the White South's attempts to erase him from history."
     One wonders "whether perhaps the author hasn't rolled back
     the gravestone and found the body arising in his novel to
     be no more or less than William Styron himself." For a
     response to this review, <u>see</u> 1968.B57.

13 ANON. "Early Styron," Dallas <u>Morning News</u> (26 May), p. 32 A.
    <u>The Long March</u> is a "splendid short novel."

14 ANON. "Six Get Honorary Degrees From Duke," Durham (N.C.) <u>Sun</u>
    (3 June), Sec. B, p. 1.
    Account of ceremony and text of Styron's degree citation.

15 ANON. "'Men...With Genius for Platitude,' He Tells Tufts Grad-
    uates--Galbraith Assails LBJ Violence Panel Members," Boston
    <u>Herald Traveler</u> (10 June), p. 3.
    Styron noted as one of five honorary degree recipients
    at Tufts University commencement. Tufts SDS chapter circu-
    lated a flier opposing awarding of degrees to Styron and
    two others, Styron's because of his "written portrayals of
    Negroes."

16 ANON. Review of <u>The Confessions of Nat Turner</u>, <u>Blackwood's
    Magazine</u>, 304 (August), 191-92.
    Although Nat "is never a credible figure," as "an evoca-
    tion of the slave condition of those times," the novel
    "shows compassion and some imaginative insight."

17 ANON. "To Honor Rose Styron--Benefit Poetry Reading," Balti-
    more <u>Sun</u> (22 November), p. B3.
    Announcement of Rose (Mrs. William) Styron's upcoming
    poetry reading and biographical and personal information
    about her and her husband.

18 APTHEKER, HERBERT. "Aptheker Defends Work Against Styron Crit-
    icism," New York <u>Times</u> (3 February), p. 27.
    Defense is based on the wide respect in which Aptheker
    claims his own work on Nat Turner is held.

19 _____. "Truth and Nat Turner: An Exchange," <u>The Nation</u>, 206
    (22 April), 543-45.
    Attack on the historical accuracy of <u>Nat Turner</u> is de-
    fended in light of charges made by Styron. See West, Item
    F 16.
    Reprinted: 1971.A2.

20 _____. "Nat Turner," <u>New York Times Book Review</u> (1 September),
    p. 10.
    Letter to the Editor defending Aptheker's works on Nat
    Turner against remarks critical of them in Martin Duberman's
    review of Clarke's <u>William Styron's Nat Turner</u>, 1968.B49.

21 ASKOUNIS, CHRISTINA. "Rose (Styron) Is a Rose Is a Poet, and
    Comes Home to Give Reading," Baltimore <u>News American</u>

1968

(4 December), Sec. B, p. 1.
News account of Mrs. Styron's return to her hometown,
Baltimore, to read from her book of children's poetry, From
Summer to Summer. Includes details on her meeting and mar-
rying Styron.

22   AYRES, B. DRUMMOND, JR. "Negro Defends Uncle Tom as Powerful
        Character," New York Times (25 February), p. 58.
            Account of speech at Howard University by Benjamin H.
        Alexander of District of Columbia School Board, a Negro,
        who expressed concern over hero status being given to Nat
        Turner, partially because of Styron's novel.

23   BAILINSON, FRANK. "Styron Answers 'Turner' Critics--In Rare
        Response, He Says He Held to 'Central Truth,'" New York
        Times (11 February), p. 59.
            Styron offers a point-by-point defense against the
        charges made by his black critics.

24   BARZELAY, DOUGLAS, and ROBERT SUSSMAN. "William Styron on
        The Confessions of Nat Turner: A Yale Lit Interview," Yale
        Literary Magazine, 137 (Fall), 24-35.
            Styron gives his reactions to the hostile reception his
        novel has received, particularly from militant Blacks.

25   BECKER, JOHN E., S.J. "Nat Turner and the Secular Humanist,"
        Review for Religious, 27 (May), 411-19.
            Nat Turner examined as one style of approach to God "cen-
        tered on withdrawal from others for personal communication
        with God."

26   BELL, BERNARD W. "The Confessions of Styron," American Dialog,
        5 (Spring), 3-7.
            The Confessions of Nat Turner is Styron's own confession
        "that he does not know Negro character nor understand Nat
        Turner" because the character of "the narrator-hero is sim-
        ply improbable and implausible" and because he has distor-
        ted history.

27   BENNETT, LERONE, JR. "The Case Against Styron's Nat Turner,"
        Ebony, 23 (October), 148-50, 154-57.
            Reprinting of Bennett's essay from Clarke's William
        Styron's Nat Turner, 1968.A1.

28   BILLINGS, CLAUDE. "Styron Views Military Psychology in
        'March,'" Indianapolis Star (5 May), Sec. 9, p. 7.
            In The Long March, "Styron writes graphic sentences and

he cuts out excess verbiage in this compact story. You
will find it hard to lay the book down once you have started
reading it."

29 BORDERS, WILLIAM. "M'Carthy Gaining in Connecticut," New York
    Times (10 March), p. 46.
        Styron listed as one of the Connecticut delegates to the
    Democratic Convention.

30 BRAXTON, PHYLLIS N., and ROBERT J. CHARLES. Letters to the
    Editor, Book World (Washington Post, Chicago Tribune) (31
    March), p. 11.
        Both letters are highly critical of Nat Turner.

31 BRENDON, PIERS. "From Jungle to Plateau," Books and Bookmen,
    13 (July), 32.
        The Confessions of Nat Turner is "a vast, imposing ba-
    roque structure, the bathos of which only becomes apparent
    when one realises that the interior is gutted, empty save
    for a few fascinating documentary knick-knacks."

32 BROWN, CECIL M. Review of The Confessions of Nat Turner, Ne-
    gro Digest, 17 (February), 51-52, 89-91.
        "One's enjoyment of the book will depend, in part, on
    his view of Civil Rights."

33 _____. Review of Clarke's William Styron's Nat Turner, Negro
    Digest, 17 (August), 91.
        Clarke's book is an "invaluable" reply to "such an un-
    just book as Styron's."

34 BRYDEN, RONALD. "Slave Rising," New Statesman, 75 (3 May),
    586-87.
        Although the "Negro is still a riddle to white America,"
    in The Confessions of Nat Turner "an attempt has been made."

35 BUCHWALD, ART. "Paper Plimpton," Playboy, 15 (January), 143,
    239.
        Humorous article in which Styron is supposedly quoted.

36 BURKMAN, KATHERINE H., ANNA MARY WELLS, STEPHEN TALLACKSON,
    GEOFFREY D. CLARK, and CAROLE A. PARKS. "Confessions Re-
    viewed," Saturday Review, 51 (13 July), 21.
        Five letters to the Editor in response to Hamilton's
    highly critical piece on Nat Turner, 1968.B70.

37 CALLANAN, KATHLEEN B. "Curl Up & Read," Seventeen, 27 (Jan-
    uary), 116.

1968

> "Reading The Confessions of Nat Turner won't change your
> world; only you can do that. But it will give you a star-
> tling new perspective on the events that are shaping your
> present and future."

38   CASEY, KEVIN. "Fiction--Act of God," Irish Times (Dublin) (18
      May), p. 8.
          Although there are passages in The Confessions of Nat
      Turner "that strike one as highly improbable if not psycho-
      logically impossible," the "total effect...is both true and
      powerful, a brilliantly imagined portrait...."

39   CHISOLM, ELISE T. "Rose Styron Is a Romantic Poet Who Listens
      to Voices of Children," Baltimore Evening Sun (4 December),
      p. B2.
          Interview in which Mrs. Styron comments on her writing
      and travelling, especially in Russia, and on racism in Amer-
      ica in light of her husband's controversial Nat Turner.

40   CLELAND, Reverend JAMES T. "Reflections on Nat Turner," The
      Whetstone (North Carolina Mutual Life Insurance Co.), 45
      (Fourth Quarter), 8-9, 26.
          Text of a sermon preached in Duke University Chapel on
      14 June 1968. Uses Styron's novel as a point of departure
      for observations on racism in American society and the
      church's view of it.

41   COLES, ROBERT. "Blacklash," Partisan Review, 35 (Winter),
      128-33.
          The Confessions of Nat Turner is "a haunting and luminous
      novel that incidentally breathes history and psychology and
      whatever on every page."

42   _____. "Arguments: The Turner Thesis," Partisan Review, 35
      (Summer), 412-14.
          Emphasizes that Styron was writing fiction not history
      and sees many black critics using Styron as a scapegoat.
      This essay is a reply to 1968.B117.

43   COLLAMORE, ELIZABETH. "Waste and Death," Hartford Courant
      (14 April), Magazine, p. 15.
          The Long March is "a very short novel--deliberately so,
      for it should be read all at once."

44   COOKE, MICHAEL. "Nat Turner's Revolt," Yale Review, 57 (Win-
      ter), 273-78.
          The Confessions of Nat Turner is "suitably mature, with-
      out a hint of self-indulgence (an apologia for the

forefathers, right or wrong), and without a hint of debil-
itating exorcism (a manifesto of innovation, forced or no)."

45 CORE, GEORGE. "Nat Turner and the Final Reckoning of Things,"
    Southern Review, 4 (Summer), 745-51.
        "The Confessions of Nat Turner not only shows that its
    author has at last found his true voice and idiom, but it
    also demonstrates that novels of the highest order can still
    be written in the South."

46 DAVIS, PAXTON. "Styron, Jarrell in New Reprints," Roanoke
    Times (5 May), p. E 14.
        The Long March is "a contemporary classic."

47 DELANY, LLOYD TOM. "A Psychologist Looks at The Confessions
    of Nat Turner," Psychology Today, 1 (January), 11-14.
        The novel lacks "the full grasp of the impact of oppres-
    sion and in spite of great effort Styron remains trapped in
    the pitfalls of American racism."

48 DRAKE, ROBERT. "Signs of the Times or Signs For All Times?"
    Christian Century, 85 (25 September), 1204-1206.
        In The Confessions of Nat Turner, "Mr. Styron has let
    his genuine concern with the news of the day overpower his
    literary judgment."

49 DUBERMAN, MARTIN. "Historical Fictions," New York Times Book
    Review (11 August), pp. 1, 26-27.
        The Confessions of Nat Turner is "superlative history."
    The specific attacks on it made in Clarke's William Styron's
    Nat Turner, here reviewed, are responded to. For a response
    to this review, see 1968.B20.
    Reprinted: 1969.B10; 1970.A1.

50 ENRIGHT, D.J. "The Caliban Story," The Listener, 79 (2 May),
    557-59.
        The Confessions of Nat Turner is "a novel, a work of
    art, a quite impressive though oppressive one."

51 F., C. A. "Military Psychology," New Orleans Times-Picayune
    (16 June), Sec. 3, p. 2.
        "As a study of military psychology,...'The Long March'
    falls far short of such works as Harry Brown's 'A Walk in
    the Sun.'"

52 FOSBURGH, LACEY. "Styron and Miller Defend Yevtushenko Against
    Charges in British Press of Hypocrisy," New York Times (25
    November), p. 15.

1968

> Styron praises Yevtushenko as "an outspoken and coura-
> geous critic of Soviet oppression."

53 FREMONT-SMITH, ELIOT. "Nat Turner I: The Controversy," New
>   York Times (1 August), p. 29.
>   Review of Clarke's William Styron's Nat Turner which ex-
>   plores the rights and responsibility of art and ideology.

54 _____. "Nat Turner II: What Myth Will Serve?" New York Times
>   (2 August), p. 31.
>   Continuation of 1968.B53 which discusses the consequences
>   of the creation and/or appropriation of myth. Expresses
>   pessimism about the ability of black and white to establish
>   a collective past.

55 FRENCH, PHILIP. "Styron and Stowe," Financial Times (London)
>   (9 May), p. 10.
>   Although The Confessions of Nat Turner is "inevitably
>   somewhat self-conscious" and "occasionally...slightly over-
>   written," it is nonetheless "in detail and overall a major
>   novel that will be read for many years to come."

56 FRIEDMAN, MELVIN J. "The Confessions of Nat Turner: The Con-
>   vergence of 'Nonfiction Novel' and 'Meditation on History,'"
>   University of Wisconsin at Milwaukee Magazine (Spring), pp.
>   3-7.
>   Abridged reprinting of Friedman's review in Journal of
>   Popular Culture, 1967.B56. See also 1970.A1 and 1974.A1.

57 FUENTES, CARLOS. "Unslavish Fidelity," Times Literary Supple-
>   ment (London) (16 May), p. 505.
>   Letter to the Editor protesting Times review of Nat
>   Turner, 1968.B12. Defends Styron's use of the first-person
>   narrator as a fictional creation and not a historical re-
>   production.

58 GELTMAN, MAX. "How Much Literary License?" National Review,
>   20 (24 September), 907.
>   The Confessions of Nat Turner is "poplit" written to
>   make the author and publisher rich.

59 GENOVESE, EUGENE D. "William Styron Before the People's
>   Court," in his Red and Black--Marxian Explorations in South-
>   ern and Afro-American History. New York: Pantheon, pp.
>   200-17.
>   Examines the ferocity and hysteria of the Negro attacks
>   on Nat Turner. Sees Styron's novel as sound historically
>   and psychologically.

60   ____. "The Nat Turner Case," New York Review of Books, 11
       (12 September), 34-37.
          Review of Clarke's William Styron's Nat Turner which de-
       fends Styron's novel on aesthetic and historical grounds.
       For a reply to this review, see 1968.B118; see also
       1968.B72, B125.
       Reprinted: 1971.A2.

61   ____. "An Exchange on 'Nat Turner,'" New York Review of Books,
       11 (7 November), 34-36.
          Insists on the heroism of Styron's Nat Turner in response
       to Styron's black critics. See also 1968.B72, B118, B125.
       Reprinted: 1971.A2.

62   GEWIRTZ, JACOB. "Black & White," Jewish Chronicle (London),
       No. 5176 (5 July), 20.
          Review of The Confessions of Nat Turner which makes no
       evaluative comment on Styron's novel but deals entirely with
       the plight of the Negro in the modern world.

63   GILMAN, RICHARD. "Nat Turner Revisited," New Republic, 158
       (27 April), 23-26, 28, 32.
          "At every moment when a religious drama might take shape
       the novelist's energy is shifted to a mere narrative of
       events, a 'story' whose own constituents, whatever their
       original existence as facts, are the stuff of melodrama."
       Reprinted: 1970.A1; 1971.A2.

64   GOODHEART, EUGENE. "When Slaves Revolt," Midstream, 14 (Jan-
       uary), 69-72.
          "Could it be that Styron wanted it both ways [in The Con-
       fessions of Nat Turner]--tragic consciousness and sympathy
       for black militancy which excludes tragic consciousness?"

65   GOODWIN, JOHN. "Bestseller Exposes Roots of Race Problem,"
       Eternity, 19 (March), 42-43.
          "Only rarely do artistic talent, historical timing and
       fundamental importance of subject matter combine to produce
       a book of unusual significance and power." The Confessions
       of Nat Turner is "such a book."

66   GREEN, MARTIN. "The Need For a New Liberalism," The Month
       (London), n.s. 40 (September), 141-47 [143-44].
          The Confessions of Nat Turner is "surely a very dull nov-
       el; its style, its narrative methods, its characterisations,
       its structure, are borrowed from Faulkner; and its central
       voice--on whose authenticity everything depends--does not
       come to life."

1968

67   GROSVENOR, PETER. "Inside the Mind of a Rebel Slave," London
     Daily Express (2 May), p. 13.
          Although The Confessions of Nat Turner is "a powerful
     tract" and Styron is "great on the set pieces of violence
     and Negro humiliation," the "narrative tends to sag under
     the outpouring of words" and "the whole thing smacks of
     twentieth century hindsight."

68   HAIRSTON, LOYLE. "William Styron's Dilemma: Nat Turner in the
     Rogues' Gallery—Some Thoughts on William Styron's Novel,
     The Confessions of Nat Turner," Freedomways, 8 (Winter), 7,
     12.
          Styron's "version of Nat Turner's 'confession' is—to put
     it bluntly—a blatant forgery; and its purpose exposes the
     author's own moral senility."

69   HALTRECHT, MONTAGUE. "A Moment of Truth in Virginia," London
     Sunday Times (5 May), p. 56.
          The Confessions of Nat Turner "is a long novel, decently
     written and with a grand narrative sweep, and can be re-
     garded as a very good class, extremely literate, version,
     with a serious subject, of your big-scale popular novel.
     Not to be sneezed at."

70   HAMILTON, CHARLES V. "Nat Turner Reconsidered: The Fiction
     and the Reality," Saturday Review, 51 (22 June), 22-23.
          Styron's conception of Nat is "mired in misinterpreta-
     tion." Emphasis on the nobility of the historical Nat
     Turner. For responses to this essay, see 1968.B36.
     Reprinted: 1968.A1.

71   HAMILTON, IAIN. "Recent Fiction," London Daily Telegraph and
     Morning Post (2 May), p. 22.
          Whether or not The Confessions of Nat Turner is a suc-
     cessful novel "depends on one's view of the imaginative
     writer's importance and relevance in particular and danger-
     ous social situations."

72   HARDING, VINCENT. "An Exchange on 'Nat Turner,'" New York Re-
     view of Books, 11 (7 November), 31-33.
          Response to Genovese's review of Clarke's William Styron's
     Nat Turner, 1968.B59. Believes that Styron fails in his at-
     tempt to understand black experience. See also 1968.B61,
     B118, B125.
     Reprinted: 1971.A2.

73   HARNACK, CURTIS. "The Quiddities of Detail," Kenyon Review, 30
     (Winter), 125-32.
          The Confessions of Nat Turner reads like "something one

1968

has read before--only this time it is done better; for while Styron gathers his imaginative powers together safely within the boundaries staked out and explored by other writers, he uses them with such energy and control that he is frequently compelling and effective."

74   HODGART, PATRICIA. "New Fiction--Tragedy and Compassion in the Deep South," Illustrated London News, 252 (18 May), 34.
       The Confessions of Nat Turner is "one of the most moving and mature novels ever written on the persistently agonizing subject of race relations."

75   HODGES, BETTY. "Betty Hodges' Book Nook," Durham (N.C.) Morning Herald (7 January), p. 5D.
       Review of Panger's Ol' Prophet Nat which compares it to Nat Turner.

76   _____. "Betty Hodges' Book Nook," Durham (N.C.) Morning Herald (3 March), p. 5D.
       Praise for Nat Turner as probable winner of upcoming National Book Award for Fiction and memories of a visit with Styron in Durham in the 1950s.

77   HOFFMAN, FREDERICK J. "The Cure of 'Nothing': The Fiction of William Styron," in Frontiers of American Culture. Edited by Ray B. Browne, Richard H. Crowder, Virgil L. Lokke, and William T. Stafford. W. Lafayette, Ind.: Purdue University Studies, pp. 69-87.
       Reprinting of 1967.B76. See also 1967.A1.

78   HOWARD, JANE. "Rose Styron," Vogue, 151 (May), 184-89, 274-75.
       Profile of and interview with Mrs. Styron, with much material on her husband and several photographs of the Styron family.

79   KAUFMANN, WALTER. "Tragedy Versus History: The Confessions of Nat Turner," in his Tragedy and Philosophy. Garden City, N.Y.: Doubleday, pp. 347-55.
       Examines the philosophical dimension of Styron's novel and finds that Styron does not begin to do justice to his theme. Nat is not tragic and is further completely unconvincing.

80   KIHSS, PETER. "Pulitzer to Styron Novel; No Prize Given For Drama," New York Times (7 May), pp. 1, 34.
       News article on awarding of Pulitzer Prizes which lists Styron as a winner for Nat Turner.

1968

81   KRUPAT, ARNOLD. "The Shock of Nat Turner," Catholic World,
      206 (February), 226-28.
          "In real life we may not seek to fathom God's reasons,
      but if we would write novels we must provide plausible mo-
      tivation even to God."

82   LEHAN, RICHARD. Review of The Confessions of Nat Turner, Con-
      temporary Literature, 9 (Autumn), 540-42.
          "While Styron's story is convincing on one level, on an-
      other level it makes a mockery of the spirit of rebellion
      and of the Negro by reducing his motives to frustrated sex."

83   LEO, JOHN. "Some Negroes Accuse Styron of Distorting Nat
      Turner's Life," New York Times (1 February), p. 34.
          Quotes Negroes for and against Nat Turner and gives
      Styron's reactions to the criticisms.

84   LISTER, RICHARD. "Brought Terrifyingly Alive--How Nat Turner
      Led the Slaves in Revolt," London Evening Standard (7 May),
      p. 10.
          The Confessions of Nat Turner is "a novel which digs deep
      into the roots of one of the worst of our present discon-
      tents. Read it, and you will understand as never before the
      howling resentment every Negro must feel deep in his heart."

*85   LUNDKVIST, ARTUR. "Vit roman om svart revolt," Dagens Nyheter
      (15 February).
          Review of The Confessions of Nat Turner.

86   MacBEATH, INNIS. "Miller Defends Yevtushenko," London Times
      (26 November), p. 5.
          Quotes Styron and Arthur Miller defending Yevtushenko
      against his British detractors.

87   McDONNELL, THOMAS P. "Novelist Shamefully Maligned By Critics,"
      The Pilot (Boston) (2 November), p. 4.
          Defense of Nat Turner against the attacks in Clarke's
      William Styron's Nat Turner.

88   McGILL, RALPH. "Astigmatic Critics--," Atlanta Constitution
      (19 February), p. 1.
          Brief defense of Styron and Nat Turner against the crit-
      ics of the novel who attack it for its "racist" and "titil-
      lating" tendencies.

89   McNEILL, ROBERT. Review of The Confessions of Nat Turner,
      Presbyterian Survey, 58 (February), 26-27.
          The novel is "fascinating and masterfully written."

90   McPHERSON, JAMES LOWELL. "America's Slave Revolt," Dissent,
      15 (January-February), 86-89.
            As long as novels like The Confessions of Nat Turner can
      be written, "the medium isn't the message. Styron's master-
      ful work rises above literary fashions, schools, and trends,
      as do the other books that we remember in our dreams."

91   MALIN, IRVING. "Nat's Confessions," University of Denver Quar-
      terly, 2 (Winter), 92-96.
            Through language, Styron in The Confessions of Nat Turner
      "manages to achieve an odd majesty that introduces and sym-
      bolizes that 'other' world in which Nat really dwells."
      Reprinted: 1970.A1.

92   _____. "Nat Turner," Catholic World, 208 (October), 43-44.
            Review of Clarke's William Styron's Nat Turner which de-
      fends Styron against his black critics while at the same
      time asserting that both Nat Turner and Clarke's book are
      "quirky, stylized, and erratic."

93   MONAGHAN, CHARLES. "Portrait of a Man Reading," Book World
      (Chicago Tribune, Washington Post) (27 October), p. 8.
            Interview in which Styron discusses his reading habits
      and preferences.

94   MOYNAHAN, JULIAN. "A Virginian Spartacus," The Observer (Lon-
      don) (5 May), p. 27.
            "While the nineteenth-century Southern rural ambience"
      of The Confessions of Nat Turner "springs thickly to life
      on many pages, Nat remains an entirely synthetic and con-
      trived character, lacking a believable voice and sensibility
      of his own."

95   MOYNIHAN, JOHN. "Fiction--Who Gets Slain? London Sunday Tele-
      graph (5 May), p. 14.
            Descriptive review of The Confessions of Nat Turner.

96   MULCHRONE, VINCENT. "The First Hot Summer of Black Power,"
      London Daily Mail (3 May), p. 10.
            The Confessions of Nat Turner is "telling, timely
      reading."

97   NEWCOMB, HORACE. "William Styron and the Act of Memory: The
      Confessions of Nat Turner," Chicago Review, 20 (No. 1), 86-
      94.
            Sees memory as a Southern preoccupation evident in all
      of Styron's novels. Nat Turner is about both Styron's mem-
      ory and the memory of the South.

1968

98   OTTAWAY, ROBERT. "Ottaway on Thursday," London <u>Daily Sketch</u>
      (2 May), p. 8.
           <u>The Confessions of Nat Turner</u> is "a thick, daunting read,
      with no moral."

99   PHIPERS, TODD. "Tedious Journey," <u>Rocky Mountain News</u> (Denver)
      (14 July), <u>Startime</u> Section, p. 19.
           Reading <u>The Long March</u> indicates that "the Styron of
      1952 simply was not the writer that the Styron of today has
      become."

100   PLATT, GERALD M. "A Sociologist Looks at <u>The Confessions of
      Nat Turner</u>," <u>Psychology Today</u>, 1 (January), 14-15.
           Styron does not convince us that "Turner's men would
      have acted as they in fact did."

101   PRICE, R. G. G. "New Fiction," <u>Punch</u>, 254 (1 May), 652.
           <u>The Confessions of Nat Turner</u> is "an immensely readable
      and exciting tour-de-force; but it strikes the British reader
      as more of a straightforward historical novel than a fiction-
      al contribution to contemporary discussion of racialism, vio-
      lence and the problem of seizing liberty by force."

102   de SAINT PHALLE, THÉRÈSE. "William Styron: 'En U.R.S.S.--et
      en France--je suis chez moi,'" <u>Le Figaro Littéraire</u> (28 Oc-
      tober-3 November), p. 26.
           Interview in which Styron speaks of Russia and Communism
      and of Faulkner and other writers.

103   SCHLUETER, PAUL. "Soul Torment," <u>Christian Century</u>, 85 (21
      February), 234-35.
           <u>The Confessions of Nat Turner</u> is "an absolute must for
      anyone interested in either literary greatness or social
      urgency."

104   SCOTT, GLENN. "Bookmarks--Battles," Norfolk <u>Virginian-Pilot</u>
      (7 April), p. C-6.
           Review of <u>The Long March</u> which consists mostly of praise
      for Styron from quoted blurbs by Dorothy Parker and Philip
      Rahv.

105   SEYMOUR-SMITH, MARTIN. "The Reality of Nat Turner," <u>The
      Scotsman</u> (Edinburgh) (11 May), <u>Week-End Scotsman</u> Section,
      p. 5.
           In <u>The Confessions of Nat Turner</u>, "there are sometimes
      faults in the writing, but these are far outweighed by the

virtues. I think we must for once go along with the pub-
lishers and agree that this book 'bears the imprint of a
classic.'"

106   SHAW, RUSSELL. Review of The Confessions of Nat Turner, Sign,
        47 (January), 63.
            "This is much more than a well-written book. It is,
        above all, a deeply moving testament to the human spirit--
        its capacity for greatness and its capacity for degradation."

107   SHEPARD, RICHARD F. "Stage and Literary Names Enlist For Can-
        didates," New York Times (14 August), p. 40.
            Notes Styron's role as co-sponsor of a fund-raising party
        for Eugene McCarthy.

108   SHRAPNEL, NORMAN. "A French Lesson," The Guardian (Manchester,
        England) (3 May), p. 7.
            The Confessions of Nat Turner is "a mournful and brutal
        novel riding on a strong surge of lyrical imagination."
        Styron has done "an eloquent job."

109   SINCLAIR, ANDREW. "Most Deliberate Revolt," New Society, 11
        (2 May), 647.
            In The Confessions of Nat Turner, "the success of Styron's
        great novel is a tribute both to his skill in his art and
        to his understanding of the corroding temper of his own
        time."

110   SITKOFF, HARVARD, and MICHAEL WRESZIN. "Whose Nat Turner:
        William Styron vs. the Black Intellectuals," Midstream, 14
        (November), 10-20.
            Sees the conflict over Styron's novel as less about the
        past than about the present.

111   SMITH, HARRY. "Bestsellers Nobody Reads," The Smith, 10 (No-
        vember), 182-84.
            A random sample of the bookbuying public reveals that
        64% of the buyers of Nat Turner have not read it, although
        all have owned it for more than a month. The median of
        pages read is 12 and less than 15% have read it fully.

112   SUDLER, BARBARA. "War Story 'The Long March' Reissued Between
        Hard Covers," Denver Sunday Post (5 May), Roundup Section,
        p. 13.
            The Long March is "a successful book with a rare, low-
        key ending that shows Styron's ability to encapsulate
        compassion."

1968

113   SUSSMAN, ROBERT. "The Case Against William Styron's <u>Nat</u>
      <u>Turner</u>," <u>Yale Literary Magazine</u>, 137 (Fall), 20-23.
            Summary of black attacks on Styron's novel and of the
      arguments of its defenders.

*114 SUYAMA, SHIZUO. "Styron no <u>The Confessions of Nat Turner</u>,"
      <u>Eigo Seinen</u> (Tokyo), 114, p. 525.
            Listed in the 1970 MLA Bibliography, Item 8261.

115   TANNER, TONY. "The Negro's Revenge," <u>The Spectator</u>, No. 7297
      (3 May), 596-97.
            "In the past Styron's prose has been marred by the curse
      of misplaced portentousness," but in <u>The Confessions of Nat</u>
      Turner, "apart from a few lapses..., he has found a subject
      adequate to his rhetoric and the result is a mature 'medi-
      tation on history' with a topical relevance which needs no
      stressing."

116   THELWELL, MICHAEL. "Mr. William Styron and the Rev. Turner,"
      <u>Massachusetts Review</u>, 9 (Winter), 7-29.
            Justifies the extra-literary criticism of <u>Nat Turner</u> and
      examines instances of arbitrary and derogatory interpreta-
      tion of history by Styron.
            Reprinted: 1968.A1; 1971.A2.

117   _____. "Arguments: The Turner Thesis," <u>Partisan Review</u>, 35
      (Summer), 403-12.
            Accuses Styron of historical distortions which cumula-
      tively "serve to present a peculiarly Southern view of black
      history not supported by the known facts." For a reply to
      this essay, <u>see</u> 1968.B42.

118   _____. "An Exchange on 'Nat Turner,'" <u>New York Review of</u>
      <u>Books</u>, 11 (7 November), 34.
            Attack on Eugene Genovese's highly critical review of
      Clarke's <u>William Styron's Nat Turner</u>, 1968.B60. <u>See also</u>
      1968.B72, B118, B125.

119   THOMAS, EMORY M. "Ten Views of the Man Who Would Not Die,"
      <u>Saturday Review</u>, 51 (17 August), 23-24.
            Review of Clarke's <u>William Styron's Nat Turner</u> which ex-
      presses opinion that Styron shows "oppression at its worst
      and rebellion at its best."

120   TURNER, DARWIN T. Review of <u>The Confessions of Nat Turner</u>,
      <u>Journal of Negro History</u>, 53 (April), 183-86.
            Styron's "major fault results from his attempts to imag-
      ine what it is like to be Negro or what it must have been

1968

like to be a slave." He also has "overemphasized the im-
pact of some forces..., and he has presented as psychological truths not only erroneous generalizations about Negroes
but also debatable speculations about human beings...."

121 TYRMAND, LEOPOLD. "Yevtushenko's Career," New York <u>Times</u> (8
December), Sec. 4, p. 13.
Letter to the Editor in response to Styron's defense of
Yevtushenko. Styron is not able to recognize "vulgar ca-
reerism disguised as spiritual independence."

122 URANG, GUNNAR. "The Voices of Tragedy in the Novels of William
Styron," in <u>Adversity and Grace: Studies in Recent American Literature</u>. Edited by Nathan A. Scott, Jr. Chicago:
University of Chicago Press, pp. 183-209.
In <u>Lie Down in Darkness</u> and <u>Set This House on Fire</u>,
Styron reinstates the tragic vision and envisions redemptive possibilities. Styron's tragedy "somehow combines the
modern equivalent of Greek objective necessity with Christian subjective responsibility."

123 VITTUM, HENRY E. "A Review," Plymouth (N.H.) <u>Record</u> (18 January), p. A6. This review also appeared in Bristol (N.H.)
<u>Enterprise</u> (28 March).
The faults of <u>The Confessions of Nat Turner</u> are "so out-
weighed by its strengths that the book is a publishing
event."

124 VIZINCZEY, STEPHEN. "America: A Fearful Fiction in Biblical
Prose," London <u>Times</u> (4 May), p. 20.
"I doubt that it is possible to write a more harebrained,
insensitive, not to say impertinent book about human suffering" than <u>The Confessions of Nat Turner</u>.

125 WELLS, ANNA MARY. "An Exchange on 'Nat Turner,'" <u>New York Review of Books</u>, 11 (7 November), 31.
Attack on Eugene Genovese's highly critical review of
Clarke's <u>William Styron's Nat Turner</u>, 1968.B60. <u>See also</u>
1968.B72, B118.

126 WHITMAN, ALDEN. "Styron Discloses Protest in Soviet--Criti-
cized Jailing of Writers During Visit to Moscow," New York
<u>Times</u> (1 November), p. 21.
News article which includes Styron's comments on the
favorable reception of <u>Nat Turner</u> in Russia and on his protest against treatment of Soviet intellectuals.

1969

1969 A BOOKS

1   LUTTRELL, WILLIAM. "Tragic and Comic Modes in Twentieth Cen-
    tury American Literature: William Styron and Joseph
    Heller." Ph.D. dissertation, Bowling Green State Univer-
    sity, 1969 [Abstracted in Dissertation Abstracts Interna-
    tional, 30 (December), 2537A].
        Styron and Heller represent tragic and comic responses,
    respectively, to a world that no longer admits to "a secure
    and stable interpretation." Perception of and rebellion
    against those forces which threaten the individual with de-
    personalization enable their heroes to transcend mere
    victimization.

2   MACKIN, COOPER R. William Styron. Southern Writers Series,
    No. 7. Austin, Texas: Steck-Vaughn, 43 pp.
        Biographical sketch and readings of the four novels as
    "Southern." Views Styron's protagonists as distinctively
    Southern rebels and notes the structural and thematic sim-
    ilarities and differences in the four novels.

*3   OLIVER, JANE SIDNEY. "Two Progressions in William Styron's
    Treatment of Minority Group Characters." M.A. thesis, Uni-
    versity of South Carolina.

1969 B SHORTER WRITINGS

1   AKIN, WILLIAM E. "Toward an Impressionistic History: Pitfalls
    and Possibilities in William Styron's Meditation on History,"
    American Quarterly, 21 (Winter), 805-12.
        Believes that Nat Turner represents the strengths and
    pitfalls of impressionistic history. Styron's Nat is em-
    phatically not an accurate portrayal of the historical Nat
    Turner, but it is very valuable to the historian.

2   ANDERSON, JERVIS. "Styron and His Black Critics," Dissent, 16
    (March-April), 157-66.
        Examines "the quality of Styron's artistic vision and
    its relevance to, or effect on the psychohistorical state
    of American society," and finds Styron's vision lacking.

3   ANON. "The Times Diary," London Times (2 April), p. 10.
        Notes producer David Wolper's announcement that he will
    consult other sources in making the film of Nat Turner.

4   BRODIN, PIERRE. "William Styron," in his <u>Vingt-cinq Améri-
     cains: Littérature & Littérateurs Américains des Années
     1960</u>. Paris: Debresse, pp. 223-26.

5   BURGER, NASH K. "Truth or Consequence: Books and Book Re-
     viewing," <u>South Atlantic Quarterly</u>, 68 (Spring), 152-66
     [155-60].
         Much of the critical acclaim for <u>Nat Turner</u> was due to
     its "reflecting the current ideological fashions of the
     Eastern liberal establishment." It perpetuates a basically
     false impression of ante-bellum Southern life, just as
     Styron's essential view of man is false.

6   COOKE, MICHAEL. "Nat Turner: Another Response," <u>Yale Review</u>,
     58 (Winter), 295-301.
         Review of Clarke's <u>William Styron's Nat Turner</u> which sees
     both <u>Nat Turner</u> and the black critics as interesting, but
     not flawless.

7   CORE, GEORGE, ed. <u>Southern Fiction Today: Renascence and Be-
     yond</u>. Athens: University of Georgia Press.
     Contents include:
     Walter Sullivan. "The New Faustus: The Southern Renascence
         and the Joycean Aesthetic," pp. 1-32 [1-5].
         Nat Turner is seen as a hero longing for death in an
         essay which looks at Southern fiction past, present, and
         future.
     Reprinted: 1972.B18.
     Louis D. Rubin, Jr. "Second Thoughts on the Old Gray Mare:
         The Continuing Relevance of Southern Literary Issues,"
         pp. 33-50 [42-43].
         <u>Nat Turner</u> shows the human values of the Southern com-
         munity in a modern context.
     George Core, C. Hugh Holman, Louis D. Rubin, Jr., and
         Walter Sullivan. "The State of Southern Fiction," pp.
         51-87 [68-69, 72-79].
         Discussion of the importance of identification with or
         detachment from the South in the case of Styron and others.
         Discussants disagree on the merits of <u>Lie Down in Darkness</u>,
         and, especially, <u>Set This House on Fire</u> and <u>Nat Turner</u>.
     George Core. "A Crossing of the Ways: An Afterword," pp.
         88-95 [94].
         <u>Set This House on Fire</u> is called typical of the Southern
         novel today; <u>Nat Turner</u> may indicate a resurgence for
         Styron and the region.

8   DAVIDSON, TED. "Countering Styron's Stereotypes," <u>Christian
     Century</u>, 86 (15 January), 89-90.

1969

Review of Clarke's <u>William Styron's Nat Turner</u>. "There
is little similarity between Styron's bumbling failure and
the man who, charged with having failed, answered only,
'Was not Christ crucified?'" Clarke's volume is a more important book than <u>Nat Turner</u>.

9   DAVIS, JOHN RODERICK. "Kuznetsov's Dilemma," New York <u>Times</u>
(27 August), p. 42.
    Letter to the Editor in response to Styron's letter (<u>see</u>
West, Item F 20) recommending that Kuznetsov not defect.
Styron's letter points up how agonizing the dilemma of the
Soviet writer is.

10 DUBERMAN, MARTIN. "William Styron's <u>Nat Turner</u> and <u>Ten Black
Writers Respond</u>," in his <u>The Uncompleted Past</u>. New York:
Random House, pp. 203-22.
    Reprinted reviews of <u>Nat Turner</u> and Clarke's <u>William
Styron's Nat Turner</u>, 1967.B44 and 1968.B49, with brief "sec-
ond thoughts" added on each piece.

11 EMMANUEL, PIERRE. "L'Histoire d'une Solitude," <u>Preuves</u>, No.
217 (April), 17-20.

12 FAUCHEREAU, SERGE. "Oncle Nat et Oncle Tom," <u>La Quinzaine
Littéraire</u>, 70 (15 April), 5-6.

13 GRESSET, MICHEL. "Les Confessions de Nat Turner: L'Histoire
Réele et le Roman-un Sociodrame Américain," <u>Preuves</u>, No.
217 (April), 3-5.

14 _____. "William Styron," <u>La Nouvelle Revue Française</u>, 204
(December), 898-907.

15 HOLDER, ALAN. "Styron's Slave: <u>The Confessions of Nat
Turner</u>," <u>South Atlantic Quarterly</u>, 68 (Spring), 167-80.
    A look at how <u>Nat Turner</u> fails as history and as liter-
ature. Styron fails to create a probable or even a possible Nat.

16 LAWSON, LEWIS A. "William Styron (1925--)," in <u>A Bibliogra-
phical Guide to the Study of Southern Literature</u>. Edited
by Louis D. Rubin, Jr. Baton Rouge: Louisiana State University Press, pp. 300-302.
    Unannotated selective listing of secondary materials,
with brief prefatory statement summarizing Styron's career.

17   LE CLEC'H, GUY. "Pour les noirs Américains la 'Confession de
      Nat Turner' n'est que celle de William Styron," Le Figaro
      Littéraire (3 March), p. 24.

18   LONG, ROBERT EMMET. "The Vogue of Gatsby's Guest List,"
      Fitzgerald/Hemingway Annual, 1, pp. 23-25 [23-24].
            Mention of Styron's use of the guest list in Lie Down in
      Down in Darkness as an echo of Fitzgerald's use of it in
      Gatsby.

19   LUKAS, J. ANTHONY. "'Om,' Ginsberg's Hindu Chant, Fails to
      Charm a Judge in Chicago," New York Times (13 December),
      p. 19.
            Summarizes Styron's testimony on two incidents of police
      brutality in course of trial of "Chicago 7."

20   MORSE, J. MITCHELL. "Social Relevance, Literary Judgment, and
      the New Right; or, The Inadvertent Confessions of William
      Styron," College English, 30 (May), 605-16.
            Nat Turner can be discussed in college classes as social
      or political fare, but it is too sloppily written to be
      discussed as a work of art.

21   NORMAND, J[EAN]. "L'homme mystifié: les héros de Bellow,
      Albee, Styron, et Mailer," Études Anglaises, 22 (October-
      December), 370-85 [378-81].

22   PICKENS, DONALD K. "Uncle Tom Becomes Nat Turner: A Commen-
      tary on Two American Heroes," Negro American Literature
      Forum, 3 (Summer), 45-48.
            Sees the resolution of the conflict between society and
      nature as central to the characters of Uncle Tom and Nat.

23   PRASAD, THAKUR GURU. "Lie Down in Darkness: A Portrait of
      the Modern Phenomenon," Indian Journal of English Studies,
      10, pp. 71-80.
            Examines Styron's novel as an aesthetic rendering of
      "the many symptoms of modernity" in theme and style.

24   RATNER, MARC L. "The Rebel Purged: Styron's The Long March,"
      Arlington Quarterly, 2 (Autumn), 27-42.
            The futility of rebellion without cause is seen as the
      theme of The Long March. This is the first of Styron's
      clear-cut novels of rebellion which culminate in the figure
      of Nat Turner.
      Reprinted: 1972.A3.

1969

25   ____. "Styron's Rebel," American Quarterly, 21 (Fall), 595–
        608.
            Study of Nat Turner which sees Styron as absorbed with
        the psychological condition of the rebel. Thus, the author
        is "primarily preoccupied with Nat Turner's psychological
        growth and secondarily with the system he opposed."
        Reprinted, in expanded form: 1972.A3.

26   RAYMONT, HENRY. "P.E.N. Congress May Discuss Censorship of
        Soviet Writers," New York Times (12 August), p. 36.
            Styron is quoted on the plight of Soviet writers: he
        agrees with Kuznetsov's denunciation of the system, but he
        fears the consequences for the liberal dissenters who re-
        mained behind.

27   ROBERTS, STEVEN V. "Over the 'Nat Turner' Screenplay Subsides
        [sic]," New York Times (31 March), p. 28.
            Pressures from the black community have forced "some
        basic changes" in the film verson of Nat Turner, according
        to producer David Wolper. Styron is said to be aware of
        the changes.

28   SALISBURY, HARRISON E. "Kuznetsov Backs Soviet on China,"
        New York Times (24 August), p. 20.
            Kuznetsov replies to Styron's view that he shouldn't
        have defected by inviting Styron to live in his (Kuznetsov's)
        vacant rooms and then see what he thinks.

29   SALOMON, MICHEL. "Interview Avec William Styron: Intolérable
        Amérique," Magazine Littéraire, 27 (March), 24–25.
            Styron talks about black power, New England, hippies,
        student movements, and the liberal intellectual community.

30   STAIR, GOBIN. "Beacon Press on Styron," Boston Globe (30
        April), p. 22.
            Letter to the Editor replying to Styron's comments in
        his April 20th interview, 1969.B33. Focus is on a defense
        of Clarke's William Styron's Nat Turner, published by Beacon
        Press and attacked by Styron in the interview.

*31   STANOVNIK, MAJDA. "Styron--Lezi v Temo," in Lezi v Temo [Lie
        Down in Darkness]. Translated by Anton Ocvirk. Ljubljana:
        Založba, Vol. 1, pp. 5–32.
            Listed in West, Item H 64.

32   SWANSON, WILLIAM J. "William Faulkner and William Styron:
        Notes on Religion," Cimarron Review, No. 7 (March), 45–52.
            Examines religion in The Sound and the Fury and Lie Down
        in Darkness. Styron "opposes the formal, ceremonial,

uncertainty-ridden religion of Carey Carr and his flock to
the irrational, bone-marrow belief of the Negro followers
of Daddy Faith."

33   TAYLOR, ROBERT. "The Contentions of William Styron," Boston
        Sunday Globe (20 April), Magazine, pp. 6-11, 13. This ar-
        ticle also appeared in Washington Post (11 May), under the
        title "The Controversies of William Styron."
            Interview in which Styron talks about black criticism of
        Nat Turner. For a response, see 1969.B30.

34   TISCHLER, NANCY M. "Negro Literature and Classic Form," Con-
        temporary Literature, 10 (Summer), 352-65.
            Focus on Nat Turner and Invisible Man. Nat is studied
        as a Black Christ, a tragic hero, and a saint.

35   WICKER, TOM. "In the Nation: What Sense in Censorship?" New
        York Times (3 April), p. 42.
            Decries the fact that black pressure "forced compromise
        upon artistic vision and purpose" in the projected film
        version of Nat Turner.

36   WOODRUF, DAVID. "Southampton County Most Likely Location For
        $4 Million Movie on Nat Turner Rebellion," Franklin (Va.)
        Tidewater News (26 September), p. 1.
            Interview with producer David Wolper about his projected
        film version of Nat Turner.

1970 A BOOKS

1   FRIEDMAN, MELVIN J., and IRVING MALIN, eds. William Styron's
        "The Confessions of Nat Turner"--A Critical Handbook.
        Belmont, Calif.: Wadsworth, 280 pp.
            This collection includes reprinted materials which help
        illuminate Styron's novel, as well as three previously un-
        published pieces. Listed below are only those items of
        literary interest which are included.
        George Plimpton. "A Shared Ordeal: Interview With William
            Styron," pp. 36-42.
                Reprinting of 1967.B124.
        Raymond A. Sokolov. "Into the Mind of Nat Turner," pp. 42-
            50.
                Reprinting of 1967.B151.
        R. W. B. Lewis and C. Vann Woodward. "Slavery In the First
            Person: Interview With William Styron," pp. 51-58.
                Reprinting of 1967.B95.

1970

Wilfrid Sheed. "The Slave Who Became a Man," pp. 59-63.
  Reprinting of 1967.B147; see also 1971.B31.
Melvin J. Friedman. "Nat Turner: A 'Meditation on His-
  tory,'" pp. 63-72.
  Reprinting of 1967.B56. See also 1968.B56.
Louis D. Rubin, Jr. "William Styron and Human Bondage,"
  pp. 72-84.
  Reprinting of 1967.B140. See also 1971.B30.
Irving Malin. "Nat's Confessions," pp. 84-88.
  Reprinting of 1968.B91.
Herbert Aptheker. "A Note on the History," pp. 89-92.
  Reprinting of 1967.B16.
Ernest Kaiser. "The Failure of William Styron," pp. 92-103.
  Reprinting of 1968.A1.
Richard Gilman. "Nat Turner Revisited," pp. 104-11.
  Reprinting of 1968.B63. See also 1971.A2.
Martin Duberman. "Historical Fictions," pp. 112-16.
  Reprinting of 1968.B49. See also 1969.B10.
Frederick J. Hoffman. "William Styron: The Metaphysical
  Hurt," pp. 126-41.
  Reprinting of 1967.B76. See also 1967.A1 and 1968.B76.
Ihab Hassan. "Encounter With Necessity," pp. 141-48.
  Reprinting of portion of 1961.B12. See also 1964.B9.
Roy Arthur Swanson. "William Styron's Clown Show," pp.
  149-64.
  Styron is a self-conscious romantic who, overwhelmed by
  Joyce and Faulkner, consistently mistakes his clown show
  for existentialist high tragedy and grand endeavor.
Karl Malkoff. "William Styron's Divine Comedy," pp. 164-
  75.
  Nat Turner deals with the same tensions Styron has de-
  veloped in his other works--between freedom and necessity,
  master and slave, father and child.
Melvin J. Friedman. "William Styron: An Interim Appraisal,"
  pp. 175-86.
  Reprinting of 1961.B9. See also 1967.A1 and 1974.A2.
Jackson R. Bryer and Marc Newman. "William Styron: A Bib-
  liography," pp. 258-80.
  Unannotated listing of material by and about Styron.
  See 1975.A4.

2   O'CONNELL, SHAUN V. "The Contexts of William Styron's The
    Confessions of Nat Turner." Ph.D. dissertation, University
    of Massachusetts, 1970 [Abstracted in Dissertation Abstracts
    International, 31 (November), 2395A].
    Explores the literary, historical, aesthetic, and polit-
    cal aspects of Nat Turner. Deals especially with the

novelist's responsibility to facts and examines Nat Turner
in light of other Southern historical fiction, other novels
about black rebellions, and Styron's other work.

1970 B SHORTER WRITINGS

1   ANON. "Teacher Is Backed in Stand on Pledge," New York Times
    (23 February), p. 24.
        Styron is among the signers of a statement supporting a
    Roxbury, Connecticut, teacher who refused to say the Pledge
    of Allegiance with her class.

2   APTHEKER, HERBERT. "Afro-American Superiority: A Neglected
    Theme in the Literature," Phylon, 31 (Winter), 336-43 [338].
        Nat Turner is cited as a monstrosity emphasizing Negro
    self-deprecation.

3   BEHAR, JACK. "History and Fiction," Novel, 3 (Spring), 260-65
    [263-65].
        The "haunting and luminous" character of Nat Turner is
    achieved "at the cost of certain kinds of bad art."

4   BONEY, F. N. "The Blue Lizard: Another View of Nat Turner's
    Country on the Eve of Rebellion," Phylon, 31 (Winter), 351-
    58 [351-52].
        Nat Turner is seen as "bold and broad, probably true in
    general terms but certainly not accurate in every detail."

5   BRYANT, JERRY H. The Open Decision--The Contemporary American
    Novel and Its Intellectual Background. New York: Free
    Press, pp. 264-68.
        Discussion of Set This House on Fire which sees in Cass
    the "affirmation of the individual for no objectively valid
    reason."

6   BULGHERONI, MARISA. "William Styron: Il Romanziere, Il Tempo
    e la Storia," Studi Americani, 16, pp. 407-28.
        In Italian.

7   CALTA, LOUIS. "Muriel Spark Calls For New Art Forms," New
    York Times (27 May), p. 40.
        Styron receives the Howells Medal for Fiction from the
    National Academy of Arts and Letters.

8   CORE, GEORGE. "The Confessions of Nat Turner and the Burden
    of the Past," Southern Literary Journal, 2 (Spring), 117-34.

1970

Sees <u>Nat Turner</u> as a historical novel. Styron is interested in the past that is in the present, rather than in
the eternally present.
Reprinted: 1975.A4.

9   CUNLIFFE, MARCUS. "Black Culture and White America," <u>Encoun-
ter</u>, 34 (January), 22-35 [29-31].
An account of "the Styron Imbroglio" as an example of
"the stifling intricacies of the comédie noire."

10 DE VECCHI ROCCA, LUISA. "Nat Turner," <u>Nuova Antologia</u>, 510
(December), 614-24.
In Italian.

11 DIPERNA, SHARON. "Portrait of a Man Reading--Joe McGinniss,"
<u>Book World</u> (Chicago <u>Tribune</u>, Washington <u>Post</u>) (3 May), p.
2.
Author of <u>The Selling of the President 1968</u> notes that
<u>Lie Down in Darkness,</u> which he's read three times, is his
favorite book: "'The people in that book...are so real and
tell so much about what it's like to live.'"

12 EPSTEIN, SEYMOUR. "Politics and the Novelist," <u>Denver Quar-
terly</u>, 4 (Winter), 1-18 [15-17].
<u>Nat Turner</u> and its reception illustrate the thesis that
novelists should stay clear of politics.

13 GEISMAR, MAXWELL. "The Shifting Illusion: Dream and Fact,"
in <u>American Dreams, American Nightmares.</u> Edited by David
Madden. Carbondale and Edwardsville: Southern Illinois
University Press, pp. 45-57 [53].
Styron is among the promising writers of the Fifties
who have disappointed. <u>Nat Turner</u> shows that he has "de-
scended to the level of a commercial best seller writer and
a romantic pseudo-historian."

14 MOERS, ELLEN. "Mrs. Stowe's Vengeance," <u>New York Review of
Books</u>, 15 (3 September), 25-32. <u>See also</u> "Nat Turner and
'Dred,'" <u>New York Review of Books,</u> 15 (19 November), 52-53.
Mention (p. 25) of Styron and <u>Nat Turner</u> in connection
with an extended discussion of Stowe's novel, <u>Dred,</u> based
in part on Nat Turner's "Confessions." Second reference is
to exchange of letters between Styron and Moers on this
essay.

15 MUDRICK, MARVIN. "Mailer and Styron," in his <u>On Culture and
Literature.</u> New York: Horizon Press, pp. 176-98.

Reprinting of Hudson Review essay, 1964.B12, with (pp. 198-99) a "Postscript 1970," commenting briefly on Nat Turner, "a compassionate and prophetic money-maker about slavery and other problematic issues."

16   NELSON, DORIS L. "The Contemporary American Family Novel: A Study in Metaphor." Ph.D. dissertation, University of Southern California, 1970 [Abstracted in Dissertation Abstracts International, 31 (December), 2929A].
   Examines the use of the family as a metaphor for some aspect of American society or for humanity in general. In Lie Down in Darkness, Styron parallels the disintegration of the Loftis family with the disintegration of values in American society.

17   RAYMONT, HENRY. "Italian Poet Gets $10,000 Prize; Styron is Cited for 'Nat Turner,'" New York Times (14 March), p. 28.
   Announcement that Styron has been awarded the Howells Medal for Fiction by the National Academy of Arts and Letters. See 1970.B7.

18   ROBB, KENNETH A. "William Styron's Don Juan," in Kierkegaard's Presence in Contemporary American Life: Essays From Various Sources. Edited by Lewis A. Lawson. Metuchen, N.J.: Scarecrow Press, pp. 177-90.
   Reprinting of 1965.B16.

19   SULLIVAN, WALTER. "Southern Writers in the Modern World: Death By Melancholy," Southern Review, n.s. 6 (Autumn), 907-19 [907-908].
   Styron listed among gifted young Southerners who have failed to fulfill the promise of early work.
   Reprinted: 1972.B18.

20   SWANSON, WILLIAM J. "Religious Implications in The Confessions of Nat Turner," Cimarron Review, No. 12 (July), 57-66.
   Examines the religious impulses of Nat Turner and charts the harsh views of ministers of orthodox Christianity.

21   TRAGLE, HENRY IRVING. "Styron and His Sources," Massachusetts Review, 11 (Winter), 134-53.
   Questions Styron's interest in the historical Nat Turner and demonstrates that Styron's research was not as thorough as he would have us believe.

22   _____. "'Credibility Gap' Seen as Reason for Change in Movie Plan," Richmond (Va.) Times-Dispatch (12 February), p. A-14.

1970

> Historian who was called in by producer of projected
> movie version of Nat Turner sees the novel as an inaccurate
> historical representation and sees the "credibility gap"
> between the novel and actual events as the major obstacle
> to making the film.

23 WATKINS, FLOYD C. The Death of Art: Black and White in the
    Recent Southern Novel. Mercer University Lamar Memorial
    Lectures, No. 13. Athens: University of Georgia Press,
    pp. 8-9, 14, 38, 57, 67.
       Uses Set This House on Fire as one illustration of the
    thesis that modern Southern novels which treat the relation-
    ship between the black man and the white man are highly
    prejudiced against the white man.

24 WEILER, A. H. "Styron Charges 'Black Pressure' on Turner Film,"
    New York Times (28 January), p. 48.
       Styron charges that the pressure comes "mostly from
    blacks who resent that a white man has written about their
    black hero."

25 WEINBERG, HELEN. The New Novel in America: The Kafkan Mode
    in Contemporary Fiction. Ithaca, N.Y.: Cornell University
    Press, pp. 124, 186, 191, 192-95, and passim.
       Set This House on Fire is referred to in several contexts:
    the spiritual quest and the theme of self-destructiveness
    are examined. Nat Turner is also seen as a spiritual quest,
    but the weight of social and political structures disqualify
    it from the Kafkan mode.

26 WIEMANN, RENATE. "William Styron: Lie Down in Darkness," Die
    Neueren Sprachen, 19 (July), 321-32.
       In German.

1971 A BOOKS

*1 DANA, PEAKE A. "Negroes in William Styron's Fiction." M.A.
    thesis, University of North Carolina.

 2 DUFF, JOHN B., and PETER M. MITCHELL, eds. The Nat Turner Re-
    bellion: The Historical Event and the Modern Controversy.
    New York: Harper & Row.
       Collection of reprinted source materials and the views
    of historians and literary critics on the historical Nat
    Turner and on Styron's novel. Includes excerpts from the
    latter and an essay by Styron. Listed below are only those
    items of literary interest which are included.

114

C. Vann Woodward. "Confessions of a Rebel: 1831," pp.
168-73.
    Reprinting of 1967.B175.
Albert Murray. "A Troublesome Property," pp. 174-80.
    Reprinting of 1967.B112.
Mike Thelwell. "Back With the Wind: Mr. Styron and the
Reverend Turner," pp. 181-90.
    Reprinting of 1968.B116. See also 1968.A1.
Herbert Aptheker. "A Note on the History," pp. 191-95.
    Reprinting of 1967.B16. See also 1970.A1.
Herbert Aptheker and William Styron. "Truth and Nat Turner:
An Exchange," pp. 195-202.
    Reprinting of 1968.B19.
Eugene D. Genovese. "The Nat Turner Case," pp. 203-16.
    Reprinting of 1968.B60.
Vincent Harding and Eugene D. Genovese. "An Exchange on
'Nat Turner,'" pp. 217-27.
    Reprinting of 1968.B72 and 1968.B61.
Richard Gilman. "Nat Turner Revisited," pp. 228-37.
    Reprinting of 1968.B63. See also 1970.A1.
Philip Rahv. "Through the Midst of Jerusalem," pp. 238-44.
    Reprinting of 1967.B128.

3   KIME, BENNA KAY. "A Critical Study of the Technique of William
    Styron." Ph.D. dissertation, Tulane University, 1971 [Ab-
    stracted in Dissertation Abstracts International, 32 (Octo-
    ber), 2058A].
        Study deals with the short stories Styron wrote prior to
    his novels and focuses on his "development of experimental
    third and first person narrative techniques."

4   MEWSHAW, MICHAEL FRANCIS. "Thematic and Stylistic Problems in
    the Work of William Styron." Ph.D. dissertation, University
    of Virginia, 1970 [Abstracted in Dissertation Abstracts In-
    ternational, 31 (March), 4727A].
        Attempts an "objective estimation of the whole body of"
    Styron's work and studies the way it contributes to the
    tradition of Southern literature, alters it for its own
    purposes, and the circumstantial changes wrought in the
    South itself. Discusses the four novels as showing a move-
    ment from "violence, doubt and despair" to an actively
    sought and sometimes forced affirmation.

5   PEARCE, RICHARD. William Styron. University of Minnesota
    Pamphlets on American Writers, No. 98. Minneapolis: Uni-
    versity of Minnesota Press. 47 pp.
        Traces Styron's "exhilarating" development as a writer
    in his four novels. Examines the tensions between Styron's

1971

belief in the traditional novel form and the world he evokes,
"where irrational warfare is the condition of life...."
Reprinted: 1974.B14.

*6 WELLS, JULIA EVANS. "Race and the Human Condition in William
Styron's The Confessions of Nat Turner." M.A. thesis, Atlanta University.

*7 WOOD, SALLY YATES. "Existentialism as Reflected in the Imagery
of William Styron's Work." M.A. thesis, University of
Richmond.

1971 B SHORTER WRITINGS

1 ANON. "Love Story," Washington Post (29 January), p. A18.
Editorial criticizing Styron and his fellow judges of
the National Book Award for Fiction for threatening to re-
sign unless the nomination of Love Story was withdrawn.
See 1971.B29.

2 ANON. "Notes on People," New York Times (21 December), p. 43.
Brief mention that Styron has completed his first play,
"In the Clap Shack," and hopes to have it produced at Yale
in the spring of 1972.

3 BEJA, MORRIS. Epiphany in the Modern Novel. Seattle: University of Washington Press, pp. 42, 150, 212-13.
Styron's work contains many frozen moments of vision; his
method is photographic.

4 BRICKHOUSE, BOB. "Styron Studied the 'Human Terms' of Slavery,"
Richmond (Va.) Times-Dispatch (15 April), pp. A1, A2.
Account of Styron lecture on slavery and Nat Turner and
interview with him about the controversy the novel has
aroused and about pending movie version.

5 BRUNAUR, DALMA H. "Black and White: The Archetypal Myth and
Its Development," Barat Review, 6 (Spring/Summer), 12-19.
Analyzes black-white imagery in an effort to discover
the roots of the equation of black=evil and white=good.
Styron provides Nat Turner with a black mythology.

6 CANNON, PATRICIA R. "Nat Turner: God, Man, or Beast?" Barat
Review, 6 (Spring/Summer), 25-28.
Analysis of New Testament parallels and images of Christ
echoed in Nat Turner. Explores the "novelty and relative

success of Styron's fiction in the stream of Bible-inspired characterizations."

7   COALE, SAMUEL CHASE, V. "The Role of the South in the Fiction of William Faulkner, Carson McCullers, Flannery O'Connor, and William Styron." Ph.D. dissertation, Brown University, 1970 [Abstracted in Dissertation Abstracts International, 31 (June), 6596A].
        "The image or role of the South changes from Faulkner to Styron and accounts for the varied styles and artistic concerns of the four writers." Styron's South is "a self-indulgent world torn between existent guilt and existential awareness."

8   COCKSHUTT, ROD. "Books: An Evening With William and Bill," Raleigh News and Observer (18 April), p. 6-IV.
        Account of an evening with Styron and Willie Morris at Duke University where, "after dinner the two of them regaled students and faculty during an informal discussion at the Duke library with serio-comic anecdotes about making it in the New York literary jungle."

9   CURTIS, BRUCE. "Fiction, Myth, and History in William Styron's Nat Turner," University College Quarterly, 16 (January), 27-32.
        Shows how Styron and his critics are both guilty of raiding the past for present-minded purposes.

10 DABNEY, VIRGINIUS. Virginia: The New Dominion. Garden City, N.Y.: Doubleday, p. 573.
        Lists Styron among Virginia's Pulitzer Prize winners.

11 FRANKLIN, JIMMIE L. "Nat Turner and Black History," Indian Journal of American Studies, 1 (November), 1-6.
        Accuses Styron's black critics of connecting "things purely political with those which are essentially aesthetic," especially in distrusting Styron's motives.

12 FRIEDMAN, MELVIN J. "William Styron," in The Politics of Twentieth-Century Novelists. Edited by George A. Panichas. New York: Hawthorn Books, pp. 335-50.
        Traces Styron's career (including his non-fiction) as disproving the "commonly held assumption that only Europeans know how to mix literature and politics." Discusses Nat Turner and recounts its tumultuous critical reception. Reprinted: 1974.A2.

1971

13 GINDIN, JAMES. <u>Harvest of a Quiet Eye: The Novel of Compassion</u>. Bloomington: Indiana University Press, pp. 349-50.
    Views <u>Nat Turner</u> as prescriptive rather than descriptive. Styron creates a respectable past for his contemporary observations.

14 GLICKSBERG, CHARLES I. <u>The Sexual Revolution in Modern American Literature</u>. The Hague: Martinus Nijhoff, pp. 200-203.
    Examination of Mason in <u>Set This House on Fire</u> as an "amoral character...who has sex on the brain," and who "bears a suspiciously close resemblance to Norman Mailer."

15 GROSS, SEYMOUR L., and EILEEN BENDER. "History, Politics and Literature: The Myth of Nat Turner," <u>American Quarterly</u>, 23 (October), 486-518.
    An attempt "to try to free Styron's novel from the coffle of propagandistic criticism masquerading as historicity so that its achievement can be more justly evaluated." Reprinted: 1975.A4.

16 HAYS, PETER L. <u>The Limping Hero--Grotesques in Literature</u>. New York: New York University Press, pp. 88-95, 166-71.
    <u>Lie Down in Darkness</u> and <u>Nat Turner</u> discussed in chapter on "Sterility Figures," <u>The Long March</u> in chapter on "Limited Man."

17 INGE, M. THOMAS. "Contemporary American Literature in Spain," <u>Tennessee Studies in Literature</u>, 16, pp. 157-66 [161].
    Styron listed among "neglected American authors who should be better known in Spain."

18 KAZIN, ALFRED. <u>Bright Book of Life--American Novelists and Storytellers From Hemingway to Mailer</u>. Boston: Little, Brown, pp. 226-28, 290-91.
    Brief discussion of <u>Nat Turner</u>; Styron fails to provide a link between the tortured self and the violent self of Nat Turner.

*19 KRETZOI, CHARLOTTE. "William Styron: Heritage and Conscience," <u>Hungarian Studies in English</u>, 5, pp. 121-36.
    Listed in 1971 MLA Bibliography, Item 9663.

20 LABRIE, RODRIGUE E. "American Naturalism: An Appraisal," <u>Markham Review</u>, 2 (February), 88-90 [90].
    Styron is one example of the legacy of naturalism; but

traditional naturalism has ended its service to more recent American fiction.

21   LUEDTKE, CAROL L.   "The Sound and the Fury and Lie Down in Darkness: Some Comparisons," Literatur in Wissenschaft und Unterricht, 4, pp. 45-51.
         Suggests that two novels resemble each other with respect to their physical and geographical settings.

22   MELLARD, JAMES M.   "Racism, Formula, and Popular Fiction," Journal of Popular Culture, 5 (Summer), 10-37 [34, 35].
         Styron's Negroes in Nat Turner are more than simple types; he uses the formula roles to cut through them to the human truths they so often conceal.

23   MELLEN, JOAN.   "Polemics--William Styron: The Absence of a Social Definition," Novel, 4 (Winter), 158-70.
         Lack of social definition in all of Styron's novels results in books about "men whose actions seem uncaused, men who are immune from social institutions and the limitations they impose, men without any dynamic connections with other human beings."

24   MULLEN, JEAN S.   "Styron's Nat Turner: A Search For Humanity," Barat Review, 6 (Spring/Summer), 6-11.
         A religious view which sees hatred as Nat Turner's religion and Jehovah as his God.

25   PEROSA, SERGIO.   "Incontri Americani," Studi Americani, 17, pp. 379-438 [389-95].
         Interview in which Styron discusses Nat Turner principally and The Long March in passing.

26   PINSKER, SANFORD.   "Christ as Revolutionary/Revolutionary as Christ: The Hero in Bernard Malamud's The Fixer and William Styron's The Confessions of Nat Turner," Barat Review, 6 (Spring/Summer), 29-37 [33-37].
         Nat envisions himself as "the mythopoeic Hero who can regenerate the barren land and lift the curse of slavery from his people."

27   [RAHV, PHILIP].   "The Editor Interviews William Styron," Modern Occasions, 1 (Fall), 501-10.
         Styron comments on the literary climate, on Jewish writers, on the novel of the day--especially the journalistic strain, and on various aspects of popular culture.

1971

28 RATNER, MARC L. "Rebellion of Wrath and Laughter: Styron's
    Set This House on Fire," Southern Review, n.s. 7 (Autumn),
    1007-1020.
        The themes of social satire and personal tragi-comedy
    are tied in Styron's novel. The latter is also compared to
    Styron's other works.
    Reprinted: 1972.A3.

29 RAYMONT, HENRY. "Book Unit Rejects 'Love Story,'" New York
    Times (22 January), p. 16.
        News item in which Styron, as member of the jury for the
    1970 National Book Award for Fiction, comments on group's
    refusal to consider Erich Segal's Love Story. For an edi-
    torial response, see 1971.B1.

30 RUBIN, LOUIS D., JR. "William Styron and Human Bondage: The
    Confessions of Nat Turner," in The Sounder Few: Essays
    From "The Hollins Critic." Edited by R. H. W. Dillard,
    George Garrett, and John Rees Moore. Athens: University
    of Georgia Press, pp. 305-17.
        Reprinting of 1967.B140, with an "Afterword" (pp. 318-23)
    which comments on the black attacks on Styron's novel.

31 SHEED, WILFRID. "William Styron: The Confessions of Nat
    Turner," in his The Morning After--Selected Essays and Re-
    views. New York: Farrar, Straus and Giroux, pp. 83-89.
        Reprinting of 1967.B147. See also 1970.A1.

32 SHEPHERD, ALLEN. "'Hopeless Paradox' and The Confessions of
    Nat Turner," Recherches Anglaises et Américaines, 4, pp.
    87-91.
        It is tragically ironic that Nat is a man, but a slave,
    that he gains his own humanity through mass execution, that
    he wishes to lead to freedom his own people who inspire con-
    tempt in him, that "he kills the only woman he has ever
    loved, and that he is ordered to execution by the only man
    who has ever truly understood him."

33 STARKE, C.J. Black Portraiture in American Fiction. New York:
    Basic Books, pp. 120, 123-25.
        Suggests that the impotence of Styron's Nat Turner as
    man and as insurrectionist takes its clue from cultural at-
    titudes toward black men.

34 TISCHLER, NANCY M. "The Confessions of Nat Turner: A Sympo-
    sium--Introduction," Barat Review, 6 (Spring/Summer), 3-4.
        Introduction to a theological consideration of Styron's
    novel.

35   VIA, DAN O., JR. "Law and Grace in Styron's <u>Set This House on Fire</u>," <u>Journal of Religion</u>, 51 (April), 125-36.
      Brief summary of theological interpretations of Styron's novel and a discussion in light of the Pauline concept of the law.

36   WHITE, JOHN. "The Novelist as Historian: William Styron and American Negro Slavery," <u>Journal of American Studies</u>, 4 (February), 233-45.
      Summarizes the racial controversy over <u>Nat Turner</u> and examines the historical biases in the book, calling it a "valuable overview."

37   WHITNEY, BLAIR. "Nat Turner's Mysticism," <u>Barat Review</u>, 6 (Spring/Summer), 21-24.
      Examines epiphanies as functional elements of plot as well as of character.

38   W[ISE], J[AMES]. "Dubious Submission & Willing Fate," <u>Duke Alumni Register</u>, 57 (November), 4-8.
      Account of Styron's appearance as a featured guest at Duke's literary festival, punctuated by a résumé of his career and by his own quoted remarks, mostly on <u>Nat Turner</u> and on his novel-in-progress, "Way of the Warrior."

1972 A BOOKS

1   CORODIMAS, PETER NICHOLAS. "Guilt and Redemption in the Novels of William Styron." Ph.D. dissertation, Ohio State University, 1971 [Abstracted in <u>Dissertation Abstracts International</u>, 32 (May), 6420A].
      "Guilt creates much of the suffering in the novels, and seems in all of them to shift from particular individuals to the world at large--a world characterized by a collective guilt which intensifies individual suffering and diminishes individual action."

2   OWNBEY, RAY WILSON. "To Choose Being: The Function of Order and Disorder in William Styron's Fiction." Ph.D. disertation, University of Utah, 1972 [Abstracted in <u>Dissertation Abstracts International</u>, 33 (September), 1176A].
      Styron's novels illustrate a search for order, mainly through violence, sex, and religion, each of which appears to a different degree in the first three novels. In <u>Nat Turner</u>, he uses all three to illustrate Nat's attempt to establish personal order.

1972

3   RATNER, MARC L. <u>William Styron</u>. Twayne's United States Au-
      thors Series, No. 196. New York: Twayne, 170 pp.
          Study of Styron's main techniques and ideas underscoring
      "the recurrent struggle of his central characters both to
      exorcise the demon of childlike egoism in themselves and to
      oppose a closed social system which regards them as vulner-
      able or rebellious children." Deals with all of the fiction
      and much of the non-fiction and sees Styron as apart from
      the Southern tradition. Parts of three chapters of this
      book appeared in previously published essays: 1969.B24;
      1969.B25; 1971.B28.

<u>1972 B SHORTER WRITINGS</u>

1   ALDRIDGE, JOHN W. "William Styron and the Derivative Imagina-
      tion," in his <u>The Devil in the Fire--Retrospective Essays</u>
      <u>on American Literature and Culture--1951-1971</u>. New York:
      Harper's Magazine Press, pp. 202-16; <u>see also</u> pp. 157-58,
      167-68.
          Reprinting of 1966.B1.

2   ANON. "New Pleas Made For Soviet Jews," New York <u>Times</u> (12
      August), p. 17.
          Styron is listed among the signers of a letter to the
      Soviet President asking the restoration of full rights for
      Soviet Jews.

3   ANON. "Styron Writes His First Play," New York <u>Times</u> (12 De-
      cember), p. 62.
          Notice of performance of "In the Clap Shack" by the Yale
      Repertory Theatre and brief remarks by Styron on the play
      and on playwriting.

4   ASKIN, DENISE. "The Half-Loaf of Learning: A Religious Theme
      in <u>The Confessions of Nat Turner</u>," <u>Christianity and Liter-</u>
      <u>ature</u>, 21 (Spring), 8-11.
          Samuel Turner leaves Nat's education dangerously unfin-
      ished since he knows through his Bible studies only a God
      of wrath, vengeance, and the sword. Margaret teaches him
      "God's love," completing his knowledge, and allowing him to
      transcend his hatred and, in this love, to save himself.

5   BARNES, CLIVE. "Stage: Playwriting Debut for Styron," New
      York <u>Times</u> (17 December), p. 67.
          "In the Clap Shack" "comes out resembling a pilot for a
      TV series....Men do not talk like this except on television

1972

series of the sixties, movies of the fifties, and plays of
the forties."

6   BOLTON, RICHARD RUSSELL. "Portrayal of the Garrison Military
    in American Fiction, 1946-1970." Ph.D. dissertation, Wash-
    ington State University, 1972 [Abstracted in Dissertation
    Abstracts International, 33 (December), 2922A].
        The Long March is among the works considered in this
    study.

7   CLARKE, GERALD. "Petronius Americanus--The Ways of Gore
    Vidal," The Atlantic, 229 (March), 44-51 [45].
        Vidal gives his opinions on Styron and his fiction--
    mostly unfavorable.

8   FRIEDMAN, MELVIN J. "William Styron and the Nouveau Roman,"
    Proceedings of the Comparative Literature Symposium (Texas
    Tech University), 5, pp. 121-37.
        Reprinting, in shortened form, of 1967.A1. See also
    1974.A2.

9   HALPERN, DANIEL. "Checking In With William Styron," Esquire,
    78 (August), 142-43.
        Interview in which Styron comments on Clifford Irving,
    Norman Mailer, Tom Wolfe, and on "In the Clap Shack."

10 HUBBELL, JAY B. Who Are the Major American Writers? Durham,
    N.C.: Duke University Press, p. 228.
        Mention of the Book Week poll (1965.B1) which listed
    Styron among the 20 American authors writing "the most dis-
    tinguished fiction during the years 1945-1965" and included
    Lie Down in Darkness among those "works of fiction written
    between 1945-1965 most memorable and likely to endure."

11 KORT, WESLEY A. "The Confessions of Nat Turner and the Dynamic
    of Revolution," in his Shriven Selves--Religious Problems
    in Recent American Fiction. Philadelphia: Fortress Press,
    pp. 116-40.
        Styron's main themes in Nat Turner are the occasion,
    sources, and goals of revolution. The other three novels
    are also examined in light of these themes.

12 KREBS, ALBIN. "Notes on People," New York Times (31 March),
    p. 14.
        Styron, Malamud, and Updike have been appointed Honorary
    Consultants at the Library of Congress for the next three
    years.

1972

13   LANDOR, MIKHAIL. "Centaur--Novels: Landor on Bellow, Updike,
      Styron and Trilling," in <u>Soviet Criticism of American Lit-
      erature in the Sixties--An Anthology</u>. Edited by Carl R.
      Proffer. Ann Arbor: Ardis, pp. 28-61 [27, 37-43, 55-59].
          This essay originally appeared in Russian and, in part,
      is a reading of <u>Set This House on Fire</u> which sees Styron
      influenced by both Faulkner and Fitzgerald and criticizes
      the "shift of the Southern novel into an existential essay."

14   MARKOS, DONALD W. "Margaret Whitehead in <u>The Confessions of
      Nat Turner</u>," <u>Studies in the Novel</u>, 4 (Spring), 52-59.
          Sexual frustration is the underlying source of motivation
      for the fictional Nat Turner. Margaret is the symbol and
      reminder of his emasculation.

15   OLDERMAN, RAYMOND M. <u>Beyond the Waste Land: A Study of the
      American Novel in the Nineteen-Sixties</u>. New Haven, Conn.:
      Yale University Press, pp. 14, 17, 95, 177.
          <u>Lie Down in Darkness</u> and <u>Set This House on Fire</u> are re-
      presentative of the American novel of the 1950s as opposed
      to that of the 1960s.

16   PETERSON, SANDRA MARNY. "The View From the Gallows: The
      Criminal Confession in American Literature." Ph.D. disser-
      tation, Northwestern University, 1972 [Abstracted in <u>Dis-
      sertation Abstracts International</u>, 33 (December), 2947A].
          <u>Nat Turner</u> is one of four major novels examined (the
      three others are <u>The Scarlet Letter</u>, <u>Billy Budd</u>, and <u>An
      American Tragedy</u>). Nat "appears to achieve salvation" but
      it is false because his method, a relationship with a white
      woman, is "incongruent with the body of his experience."

17   SARADHI, K. P. "The Agony of a Slave Negro: Theme and Tech-
      nique in Styron's <u>Nat Turner</u>," <u>Osmania Journal of English
      Studies</u>, 9 (No. 1), 11-19.
          Views <u>Nat Turner</u> as flawed by a "lack of proper dramatic
      motivation." Suggests that Styron's problems are caused
      by "a lack of proper understanding of the Negro personality."
      Reprinted: 1975.B11.

18   SULLIVAN, WALTER. <u>Death By Melancholy: Essays on Modern
      Southern Fiction</u>. Baton Rouge: Louisiana State University
      Press, pp. 66, 67, 87, 88, 97-102, 115.
          This material is reprintings of previously published
      essays, 1969.B7 and 1970.B19.

1973 A BOOKS

1 MORGAN, HENRY GRADY, JR. "The World as Prison: A Study of
   the Novels of William Styron." Ph.D. dissertation, University of Colorado, 1973 [Abstracted in <u>Dissertation Abstracts
   International</u>, 34 (October), 1924A].
      Each of Styron's protagonists "must find a <u>raison d'être</u>
   even within the confines of...bondage." Each protagonist is
   similar to the others in suffering a sense of imprisonment,
   but the characters in the later novels find "affirmative
   values which validate existence." All four novels are
   discussed.

2 STRINE, MARY SUSAN. "The Novel as Rhetorical Act: An Interpretation of the Major Fiction of William Styron." Ph.D.
   dissertation, University of Washington, 1972 [Abstracted in
   <u>Dissertation Abstracts International</u>, 33 (June), 7067A].
      "The purpose of this study is to explicate the novels of
   William Styron as a cumulative sequence of implicitly rhetorical acts whereby strategic responses are made to the
   socio-psychological conditions of mid-twentieth century
   American life." All four novels are discussed.

3 SWANSON, WILLIAM JOSEPH. "William Styron, Eloquent Protestant."
   Ph.D. dissertation, University of Northern Colorado, 1972
   [Abstracted in <u>Dissertation Abstracts International</u>, 33
   (January), 3676A].
      "This study attempts to demonstrate that William Styron
   is not only a protest writer, but an 'unconventional' protest writer: one who employs the rhetoric of the tradition-
   alist (rhetoric that is characterized by long, carefully
   constructed sentences, poetic diction, and copious literary
   allusions)." Deals with the four novels.

1973 B SHORTER WRITINGS

1 ANON. Review of <u>In the Clap Shack</u>, <u>Publishers' Weekly</u>, 203
   (7 May), 63.
      "Styron shows a real theatrical flair, playing barracks
   humor against raw human drama."

2 ANON. Review of <u>In the Clap Shack</u>, Washington <u>Post</u> (15 July),
   <u>Book World</u>, p. 15.
      Styron depicts the VD ward "with an observant eye"; the
   locale is "suitably exploited for ribald humor and wry reflections on the human condition."

1973

3   ANON. "Martha's Troubled Vineyard," Time, 102 (30 July), 42-
    43.
        Brief mention of Styron's support for a bill introduced
    by Senator Edward Kennedy limiting building on and commer-
    cialization of Martha's Vineyard.

4   ANON. "Notes on People," New York Times (10 November), p. 37.
        Short news item reporting that Styron and others have
    purchased a large tract of land in Connecticut.

5   BROCKWAY, JODY. Review of In the Clap Shack, Theatre Crafts,
    6 (June), 44.
        One-sentence mention: it is "a fine play."

6   BROWN, ASHLEY. "Red Leaves," New York Times Book Review (1
    July), p. 24.
        Letter to the Editor, pointing out that Styron's conten-
    tion, made in his review of Malcolm Cowley's A Second Flow-
    ering (West, Item E 74), that Faulkner's "Red Leaves" was
    influenced by Hemingway's Death in the Afternoon, is ren-
    dered dubious by the fact that the latter was not published
    until two years after Faulkner's story.

7   BUSHNELL, NINA. "The Quest For Nat Turner," Newport News (Va.)
    Daily Press (27 April), p. 13.
        Interview in which Styron speaks of his childhood in
    Newport News, of the origins of Nat Turner, and of Negroes.

8   FUSSELL, B. H. "On the Trail of the Lonesome Dramaturge,"
    Hudson Review, 26 (Winter), 753-62 [745].
        Brief mention of In the Clap Shack: "The overwhelming
    fatigue engendered, I suspect, in the author as well as in
    the audience, by the formulaic characters, situations, con-
    flicts...makes this play no more than a crapula of the
    night before."

9   GOODWYN, WRENDA. "William Styron Remembers Past," Newport
    News (Va.) Times-Herald (26 May), p. 6S.
        Interview in which Styron reminisces about his childhood
    in Newport News and comments on the modern South.

10 HASSAN, IHAB. Contemporary American Literature 1945-1972: An
    Introduction. New York: Frederick Ungar, pp. 54-56.
        Introductory remarks on Styron and his fiction: he lacks
    "a felt attitude toward life, a distinctive power of
    evaluation."

11   KOCHANEK, PATRICIA SHARPE. "In Pursuit of Proteus: A
     Piagetian Approach to the Structure of the Grotesque in
     American Fiction of the Fifties." Ph.D. dissertation,
     Pennsylvania State University, 1972 [Abstracted in <u>Disser-
     tation Abstracts International</u>, 33 (April), 5729A-30A].
       Deals with <u>Lie Down in Darkness</u> and <u>Set This House on
     Fire</u>.

12   LEON, PHILLIP W. "Styron Publishes First Play," Nashville <u>Ten-
     nessean</u> (2 September), p. 10-E.
       "The black humor does not obscure the serious, even pa-
     thetic description of the human dilemma. Only the most
     flint-skinned reader will fail to sympathize...."

13   LEONARD, MARY ANNE. "NN Life Set Styron on Pulitzer Path,"
     Newport News (Va.) <u>Times-Herald</u> (28 April), p. 20.
       News story on talk given by Styron at Old Dominion Uni-
     versity in which he comments about the reception of <u>Nat
     Turner</u> and about the modern South.

14   NOLTE, WILLIAM H. "Styron's Meditation on Saviors," <u>Southwest
     Review</u>, 58 (Autumn), 338-48.
       Nat Turner is no revolutionary but rather "a highly
     strung and neurosis-driven savior." Styron's novel is an
     analysis of "the savior complex."

15   OATES, STEPHEN B. "Children of Darkness," <u>American Heritage</u>,
     24 (October), 42-47, 89-91 [91].
       An historical account of the real Nat Turner, followed
     by a brief note which calls Styron's novel "an inaccurate
     and unacceptable recreation of Turner and his insurrection."

16   PERRY, J. DOUGLAS, JR. "Gothic as Vortex: The Form of Horror
     in Capote, Faulkner, and Styron," <u>Modern Fiction Studies</u>,
     19 (Summer), 153-67.
       Examines Styron's adaptation of gothic methods and form
     in <u>Set This House on Fire</u>. All three writers document "a
     sense of the void at the center of things, a conviction
     that chaos is about to rise up and swallow man's personal
     order." For Styron, this is manifested when "one person
     tries to establish himself in terms of his relations to
     others."

17   PEYRE, HENRI. "Is Literature Dead? Or Dying?" <u>Michigan
     Quarterly Review</u>, 12 (Fall), 297-313 [301, 303].
       Styron "may still assume the outstanding if solitary
     role of the most daring and forceful novelist of his

1973

        generation"; but his maturation process has been very slow
and his themes are monotonous.

18   SINK, D. MICHAEL. "A Response to Critics--The Confessions of
        Nat Turner," Clearing House, 48 (October), 125-26.
            Nat Turner is "a first-rate book" and "a good novel" be-
cause "it is a highly-crafted creation (not a history) that
deals with a segment of the human condition its author obviously considered significant." As an artist, Styron was
"bound by no rules which say he must write this way or that,
or treat his subject matter in a prescribed posture."

19   SPEARMAN, WALTER. Review of In the Clap Shack, Chapel Hill
        (N.C.) Weekly (8 July), p. 4-C.
            "The language is as unrestrained as one would expect
from a Navy VD ward and the human elements of the drama are
made extremely dramatic. Able acting would probably make
the characters more convincing than they seem in the exag-
gerated black-and-white portrayals of almost inhuman
individuals."

20   VANDERBILT, KERMIT. "Writers of the Troubled Sixties," The
        Nation, 217 (17 December), 661-65 [661, 664].
            Nat Turner is one of eight books discussed. Styron's
novel anticipated "the reservations that now characterize
our response to the whole decade."

21   WILD, FREDRIC MAX, JR. "'A Plank in Reason': Time, Space and
        the Perception of the Self in the Modern Novel." Ph.D.
        dissertation, Ohio State University, 1973 [Abstracted in
        Dissertation Abstracts International, 34 (November), 2665A].
            Examines Lie Down in Darkness as an "existential" novel
which perceives self as "a divided being, unable to make
contact with the past or with the future and to account for
itself in a historical way."

1974 A BOOKS

1   CHESHIRE, ARDNER R., JR. "The Theme of Redemption in the Fic-
        tion of William Styron." Ph.D. dissertation, Louisiana
        State University, 1973 [Abstracted in Dissertation Abstracts
        International, 35 (August), 1089A-90A].
            Styron implies that man is always having to modify or
change his values in the light of experience. Thus, his
"redemptive endings" seem forced.

2   FRIEDMAN, MELVIN J. <u>William Faulkner</u>. Popular Writers Series,
    No. 3. Bowling Green, Ohio: Bowling Green University Pop-
    ular Press, 72 pp.
        Examines Styron's literary debts to Faulkner, Hemingway,
    Proust, Camus, and Fitzgerald and describes his kinship
    thematically and technically with contemporary French fic-
    tion writers. Also discusses and documents the receptions
    of Styron's novels and includes a look at his novel-in-
    progress, "The Way of the Warrior." Much of this material
    appeared in earlier essays, 1961.B9; 1972.B8; 1971.B12;
    1967.B57. <u>See also</u> 1967.A1; 1970.A1; 1968.B55.

3   LAXMANA MURTHY, S. "The Novels of William Styron--An Existen-
    tial Study." M. Litt. thesis, Osmania University Post-
    Graduate Centre, Warangal, India.
        "My attempt here has been to indicate through the anal-
    ysis of all four of Styron's novels a progression in his
    thought from the Kierkegaardian 'leap of faith' to the
    Camusian affirmation." A copy of this thesis is in the
    Styron collection at the Duke University library.

1974 B SHORTER WRITINGS

*1 ANON. "Chętnie Się Zapomina O Ludzkiej Niedoli: Rozmowa z
    Williamem Styronem," <u>Literatura</u> (Warsaw) (11 April).
        Interview in which Styron talks about the Vietnam War,
    his novel-in-progress ("Sophie's Choice"), and the "Ameri-
    can Dream." Listed in West, Item I 75.

2   BROWNING, PRESTON M., JR. "The Quest For Being in Contempo-
    rary American Fiction," <u>Forum</u> (Houston), 12 (Spring), 40-
    46 [41].
        The theme of being as a diminished or lost potential is
    dramatized in <u>Lie Down in Darkness</u>.

3   DOMMERGUES, PIERRE. "William Styron à Paris," <u>Le Monde</u> (26
    April), pp. 19, 26.
        Interview in which Styron speaks of the South, <u>Nat
    Turner</u>, Faulkner, and of his novel-in-progress, "Sophie's
    Choice."

4   EGGENSCHWILER, DAVID. "Tragedy and Melodrama in <u>The Confes-
    sions of Nat Turner</u>," <u>Twentieth Century Literature</u>, 20
    (January), 19-33.
        Consideration of <u>Nat Turner</u> in light of the varied re-
    sponses of previous critics. Styron "depicts a destructive
    attempt to hide from a surmountable tragic vision of life."

1974

5   FORKNER, BEN, and GILBERT SCHRICKE. "An Interview With William
    Styron," Southern Review, n.s. 10 (Autumn), 923-34.
        Topics include Nat Turner and Styron's novel-in-progress,
    "Sophie's Choice." Styron relates his latest work to themes
    in Lie Down in Darkness.

6   HAVIRD, DAVID. "Novelist Styron Pays Social Visit," The
    Gamecock (University of South Carolina, Columbia, S.C.)
    (28 January), pp. 4, 7.
        Report, with quotations, on Styron's guest appearance in
    James Dickey's seminar at the University of South Carolina.
    Among the topics discussed are Southern writing and writers,
    the reception of Nat Turner, Faulkner, and the writing
    process.

7   HEINEY, DONALD, and LENTHIEL H. DOWNS. Recent American Liter-
    ature After 1930. Essentials of Contemporary Literature of
    the Western World, Vol. 4. Woodbury, N.Y.: Barron's Edu-
    cational Series, pp. 264-68.
        Brief survey of Styron's life and writings, with plot
    summaries of the novels and excerpts from critical commen-
    taries on Styron's fiction.

8   HENDERSON, HARRY B., III. "The Fixer and The Confessions of
    Nat Turner: The Individual Conscience in Crisis," in his
    Versions of the Past: The Historical Imagination in Amer-
    ican Fiction. New York: Oxford University Press, pp. 273-
    77.
        Nat Turner is "evidence of the contemporary liberal
    amidst renewed conflict in American society." Nat is the
    "psychologically warped victim of a racist society."

9   HIERS, JOHN TURNER. "Traditional Death Customs in Modern
    Southern Fiction." Ph.D., Emory University, 1974 [Abstract-
    ed in Dissertation Abstracts International, 35 (August),
    1103A].
        Lie Down in Darkness is one example of many Southern
    novels and short stories which illustrate "the rural South's
    plethora of traditional death customs and rituals" which
    help characters learn "self-definition" and "primal sympa-
    thy for one's brothers."

10 HOERCHNER, SUSAN JANE. "'I Have to Keep the Two Things Sepa-
    rate': Polarity in Women in the Contemporary American
    Novel." Ph.D. dissertation, Emory University, 1973 [Ab-
    stracted in Dissertation Abstracts International, 34 (May),
    7233A].
        "In the contemporary American novel, the social woman

denies the flesh simply because she fears or hates the body," and she becomes a "destructive force" who may "wreak havoc" on those around her--like Helen Loftis in Lie Down in Darkness.

11   MALIN, IRVING. "Styron's Play," Southern Literary Journal, 6 (Spring), 151-57.
        Detailed scene-by-scene explication of In the Clap Shack. Although "inferior to Styron's best fictions," it deals "with universal patterns of meaning--with the nature of freedom (rebellion against authority) and the quality of language." It is "primarily a didactic work, sublimating character and plot to theme, but it still works powerfully at times--especially in the ironic, 'accidental' turn of final events."

12   MORTON, JAMES PARKS, EDITH WYTHOSGROD, ROSEMARY RUETHER, MICHAEL D. RYAN, and IRVING GREENBERG. "Auschwitz Sympo- sium: Reply to a Critic," New York Times (25 July), p. 40.
        Responses to Styron's article, "Auschwitz's Message" (West, Item E 78).

13   NORMAND, JEAN. "'Un lit de ténèbras' de W. Styron: Variations sur le thème de Tristan," Études Anglaises, 27 (January- March), 64-71.

14   PEARCE, RICHARD. "William Styron--1925-," in American Writ- ers--A Collection of Literary Biographies. Edited by Leonard Unger. New York: Charles Scribner's Sons, Vol. IV, pp. 97-119.
        Reprinting of 1971.A5.

15   SULLIVAN, JEREMIAH J. "Conflict in the Modern American Novel," Ball State University Forum, 15 (Spring), 28-36 [33-34].
        The conflict in Nat Turner is Dreiser's "natural impulse, in this case for freedom, against the unnatural slave code, [which] may lead to horrible consequences for both hero and society."

1975 A BOOKS

1   FIRESTONE, BRUCE M. "A Study of William Styron's Fiction." Ph.D. dissertation, University of North Carolina, Chapel Hill, 1975 [Abstracted in Dissertation Abstracts Interna- tional, 36 (December), 3684A-85A].
        Much of the meaning of Styron's fiction derives from the

1975

interaction between what is being told and the process of telling.

2   GOODLEY, NANCY C. "All Flesh Is Grass: Despair and Affirmation in Lie Down in Darkness." Ph.D. dissertation, American University, 1975 [Abstracted in Dissertation Abstracts International, 36 (September), 1496A].
        Lie Down in Darkness, although it contains existential themes, is strongly affirmative and Christian. Styron uses conventional literary forms and theological models to underscore his message.

3   LEON, PHILIP W. "Idea and Technique in the Novels of William Styron." Ph.D. dissertation, George Peabody College for Teachers, 1974 [Abstracted in Dissertation Abstracts International, 35 (June), 7911A-12A].
        Examines the central themes of the four novels and the devices Styron uses to convey them.

4   MORRIS, ROBERT K., and IRVING MALIN, eds. The Achievement of William Styron. Athens: University of Georgia Press, 280 pp.
    Contents:
    Robert K. Morris and Irving Malin. "Vision and Value: The Achievement of William Styron," pp. 1-23.
        Sees Styron's works as studies of "characters who, despite their realization of the abyss, are willing out of the sense of an ultimate motive and purpose in life to challenge it."
    Robert K. Morris. "An Interview With William Styron," pp. 24-50.
        Topics include problems he experienced in writing each of his novels, his protagonists, his Southern origins, the production of "In the Clap Shack," his novel-in-progress ("The Way of the Warrior"), and Styron's experiences as a teacher of writing.
    Louis D. Rubin, Jr. "Notes on a Southern Writer in Our Time," pp. 51-87.
        Reprinting of 1963.B22.
    John O. Lyons. "On Lie Down in Darkness," pp. 88-99.
        Sees the novel as less than tragic and notes that Styron's style obscures what it tries to make clear.
    Jan B. Gordon. "Permutations of Death: A Reading of Lie Down in Darkness," pp. 100-21.
        Styron's novel is about the relationship between life in death and death in life and explores the consequences of the equation of love with need.

Irving Malin. "The Symbolic March," pp. 122-33.
Examines symbols, themes, and characters in The Long
March. The three main characters are explored in depth
as key to the novel.
Robert Phillips. "Mask and Symbol in Set This House on
Fire," pp. 134-49.
Rejects a tragic interpretation of the novel and uses
its symbolism as a clue to its many layers of meaning.
George Core. "The Confessions of Nat Turner and the Burden
of the Past," pp. 150-67.
Reprinting of 1970.B8.
Seymour L. Gross and Eileen Bender. "History, Politics,
and Literature: The Myth of Nat Turner," pp. 168-207.
Reprinting of 1971.B15.
Norman Kelvin. "The Divided Self: William Styron's Fiction
From Lie Down in Darkness to The Confessions of Nat
Turner," pp. 208-26.
Styron attempts to invoke a romantic vision out of re-
alistic details in dealing with the meaning and action of
evil. All four novels are examined in light of this
thesis.
Robert K. Morris. "In the Clap Shack: Comedy in the
Charnel House," pp. 227-41.
Styron resurrects "from the tragic fact of death the
human comedy and purpose of life."
Jackson R. Bryer. "William Styron: A Bibliography," pp.
242-77.
Expanded version of 1970.A1.

1975 B SHORTER WRITINGS

1   AICHINGER, PETER. The American Soldier in Fiction, 1880-1963:
A History of Attitudes Toward Warfare and the Military Establishment. Ames: Iowa State University Press, pp. 44,
46, 51, 56, 61, 67-68, 89-90, 103.
Examines Styron's anti-military stance in The Long March.

2   ANON. "For Bill Styron, It's Work, Tennis, Parties," People,
4 (21 July), 7.
Picture of Styron with brief caption in picture-story
on famous residents of Martha's Vineyard.

3   ANON. "Styron Addresses 1975 Graduates," The Stingaree:
Christchurch Student Alumni News, 55 (Summer), 1.
Account of Styron's commencement speech at the 1975
graduation exercises at Christchurch School. See 1977.B15.

1975

4   ANON. "Three Fights For Justice," Time, 106 (29 December), 32.
        Styron, Arthur Miller, and others are attempting to re-
    open the case of a Connecticut teenager convicted of man-
    slaughter in 1973.

5   BILOTTA, JAMES D. "Critique of Styron's Confessions of Nat
        Turner," Negro History Bulletin, 38 (December 1974-January),
        326-27.
            Summary of responses to Nat Turner. Styron's "problem"
        may lie "with his view of history. How can one wish to vary
        from historical fact in order to produce a much more total
        historical faithfulness?"

6   GAYLE, ADDISON, JR. The Way of the New World--The Black Novel
        in America. Garden City, N.Y.: Anchor Press/Doubleday,
        pp. 234-37.
            Nat Turner is "counter-history" and "the product of a
        white man lacking the courage to confront history as revealed
        fact; one who must, instead, deal with it as fable and myth
        in an attempt to sanction the image of the 'good, loyal
        darky.'"

7   GRAY, RICHARD. "Victims and History and Agents of Revolution:
        An Approach to William Styron," Dutch Quarterly Review of
        Anglo-American Letters, 5 (No. 1), 3-23.
            In the largely autobiographical Lie Down in Darkness,
        Styron depends on the early literary traditions of the South.
        The Long March and Set This House on Fire mark no advance;
        but in Nat Turner he offers a revolutionary new look at the
        Southern past.
        Reprinted: 1977.B7.

8   HIERS, JOHN T. "The Graveyard Epiphany in Modern Southern
        Fiction: Transcendence of Selfhood," Southern Humanities
        Review, 9 (Fall), 389-403 [400-401].
            Styron, along with Agee, O'Connor, Wolfe, Welty, and
        Humphrey, is studied, with emphasis on Lie Down in Darkness,
        which shows "no redemption whatsoever in death."

*9 NENADAL, RODOSLAV. Untitled note, in Zapal Tento Dum [Set This
        House on Fire]. Prague: Odeon, pp. 483-91.
            West, Item H 10.

10 O'CONNELL, SHAUN. "William Styron: In the Refracted Light of
        Reminiscence," Boston Sunday Globe (27 April), Magazine, pp.
        30, 32-39.
            Interview in which Styron speaks of his summer home on
        Martha's Vineyard, of his novel-in-progress ("Sophie's
        Choice"), and of a boyhood meeting with Eleanor Roosevelt.

11   SARADHI, K. P. "The Agony of a Slave Negro: Theme and Tech-
      nique in Styron's Nat Turner," Literary Half-Yearly, 16
      (January), 41-51.
            Reprinting of 1972.B17.

12   SAUDER, RON. "Styron Recalls Days at Christchurch," Richmond
      (Va.) Times-Dispatch (25 May), pp. A-1, A-2.
            Styron reminisces about his high school years.

13   SHAPIRO, HERBERT. "The Confessions of Nat Turner: William
      Styron and His Critics," Negro American Literature Forum,
      9 (Winter), 99-104.
            Reviews the criticism of Nat Turner and finds Styron
      guilty of "hasty and exaggerated" historical judgments. He
      fails to separate the Sambo stereotype from other patterns
      of slave resistance and inaccurately stresses the futility
      of the result.

14   TROCARD, CATHERINE. "William Styron and the Historical Novel,"
      Neohelicon, 3 (No. 1-2), 373-82.
            Lie Down in Darkness must be considered "part fiction, part
      history, part autobiography, part psychology." It is a study
      of modern despair, realistic in setting and psychology.

15   WEST, JAMES L. W., III. "A Bibliographer's Interview With
      William Styron," Costerus, n.s. 4, pp. 13-29.
            Styron speaks about his writing habits, his attitude to-
      wards his texts, and his relationships with his editors.
      Includes facsimiles of manuscripts, typescripts, and galleys.

16   _____, ed. "William Styron's Afterword to The Long March,"
      Mississippi Quarterly, 28 (Spring), 185-89.
            First English version of Styron's brief description of
      the novel's composition and of circumstances out of which
      it grew, originally published in Norwegian translation of
      the novel, is prefaced by a brief introductory note.

1976 A BOOKS

1   ANON. An Exhibition--William Styron in Mid-Career. William
      R. Perkins Library--Duke University--15 March-15 April 1976.
            Catalogue of Duke University Library exhibition of Styron
      materials.

2   LANG, JOHN DOUGLAS. "William Styron: The Christian Imagina-
      tion." Ph.D. dissertation, Stanford University, 1975 [Ab-
      stracted in Dissertation Abstracts International, 36 (March),
      6101A].

1976

> In <u>Lie Down in Darkness</u>, <u>Set This House on Fire</u>, and <u>Nat</u>
> <u>Turner</u>, Styron deals with "the decay of personal, social,
> and religious values and with the need for a 'renewed under-
> standing of the moral and spiritual dimensions of human
> existence,' which are best seen in the individual's under-
> standing his position as <u>imago dei</u>." <u>The Long March</u> and <u>In</u>
> <u>the Clap Shack</u> are also considered.

3   MILLS, EVA BAMBERGER. "The Development of William Styron's
     Artistic Consciousness: A Study of the Relationship Between
     Life and Work." Ph.D. dissertation, University of Cincin-
     nati, 1976 [Abstracted in <u>Dissertation Abstracts Interna-</u>
     <u>tional</u>, 37 (November), 2874A–75A].
         Describes and traces the influence of the life of William
     Styron on his work by "emphasizing the <u>formal</u> relationship
     between significant events in his life and in the world;
     and the ethical beliefs, opinions and attitudes revealed in
     his non-fictional writings and in his public statements; and
     all of these as they appear in his novels."

<u>1976 B SHORTER WRITINGS</u>

1   CHESHIRE, ARDNER R., JR. "The Recollective Structure of <u>The</u>
     <u>Confessions of Nat Turner</u>," <u>Southern Review</u>, n.s. 12 (Winter),
     110–21.
         Sees the recollective character of the hero dependent on
     past experience as the structural key to the novel. Through
     recollection, Nat transcends "the voids of submission to
     faith and solipsism" and achieves redemption.

2   EDMISTON, SUSAN, and LINDA D. CIRINO. <u>Literary New York--A</u>
     <u>History and Guide</u>. Boston: Houghton Mifflin, pp. 97–98,
     109.
         Brief mention of Styron's stays in New York during 1947
     and 1949, while he was writing <u>Lie Down in Darkness</u>.

3   FLANDERS, JANE. "William Styron's Southern Myth," <u>Louisiana</u>
     <u>Studies</u>, 15 (Fall), 263–78.
         In his three long novels, Styron develops a "coherent
     view of Southern history" which contains "a religious at-
     titude, insistently aware of irrationality and evil" but
     which nonetheless clings "to an ideal of moral harmony."
     Nat is the culmination of Styron's Southern myth, which be-
     gins in "shame and despair" in <u>Lie Down in Darkness</u>, but
     arrives at a "tentative but growing optimism" in <u>Nat Turner</u>
     by suggesting Styron's "hope for the reconciliation of
     peoples whose separation has blighted Southern history."

4   FUENTES, CARLOS. "William Styron in Mexico," tr. by Margaret
    Peden, <u>Review</u>, 17 (Spring), 67-70.
        Styron's novels "are like bridges that unite history and
    tragedy across the abysses of the personal." In <u>Nat Turner</u>,
    he creates "a new and a true present." This essay is ex-
    cerpted from <u>Casa con dos puertas</u>. Mexico: Editorial
    Joaquin Mortiz, 1970.

5   G[EOFFREY], N[ORMAN]. "Backstage With Esquire," <u>Esquire</u>, 86
    (September), 38.
        Column includes comments by Styron on "Sophie's Choice"
    and "The Way of the Warrior."

6   LEON, PHILIP W. "<u>The Lost Boy</u> and a Lost Girl," <u>Southern Lit-
    erary Journal</u>, 9 (Fall), 61-69.
        Traces influence on <u>Lie Down in Darkness</u> of Thomas Wolfe's
    "The Lost Boy" (chapter 5 of <u>Look Homeward, Angel</u>).

7   LOBIONDO, JOAN. "William Styron: Learning From Past?" Danbury
    (Conn.) <u>News-Times</u> (4 July), pp. A-1, A-10.
        Interview in which Styron talks about Jimmy Carter, racial
    problems, foreign policy, and America's past.

8   McGINNISS, JOE. <u>Heroes</u>. New York: Viking Press, pp. 64-70.
        Account of visit to Styron at his summer home on Martha's
    Vineyard.

*9   OKOGBUE, C. "The Negro Slave and 'Black-Assed' Feeling in
    American Fiction," <u>Muse</u> (Nsukka), 8, pp. 57-60.
        Listed in 1976 MLA Bibliography, Item 11392.

10   ROSE, ALAN HENRY. <u>Demonic Vision--Racial Fantasy and Southern
    Fiction</u>. Hamden, Conn.: Archon Books, p. 128.
        Brief mention of symbolic use of Negro religion in <u>Lie
    Down in Darkness</u>.

11   SULLIVAN, WALTER. <u>A Requiem For the Renascence--The State of
    Fiction in the Modern South</u>. Athens: University of Geor-
    gia Press, pp. xxii-xxiii, 24, 70.
        Scattered brief mention of Styron. Some of this material
    is reprinted from 1964.B16.

12   UYA, OKON E. "Race, Ideology and Scholarship in the United
    States: William Styron's <u>Nat Turner</u> and Its Critics,"
    <u>American Studies International</u>, 15 (Winter), 63-81.
        Summarizes issues and questions raised concerning <u>Nat
    Turner</u> by black writers and historians. The novel is "a
    tragic love story...on one level: the passion of killing

1976

and the passion of love create a dichotomy which does work together....there is a potential romance here, aborted by the circumstance of slavery." Styron's deviations from history are defensible because "to create effective litera- ture one must fashion and manipulate the world, control it, and hence, create meaning out of chaos."

13 WILLIAMS, ERNEST P. "William Styron and His Ten Black Critics: A Belated Meditation," Phylon, 37 (June), 189-95.
    Black critic takes issue with contributors to Clarke's William Styron's Nat Turner, conceding that essayists jus- tifiably find Styron offensive in asserting that slaves were satisfied with slavery and were "too docile and spiritless to protest"; but pointing out that many of Styron's details can be documented through non-racist documents here cited.

1977 A BOOKS

1 ARMS, VALARIE MELIOTES. "William Styron's Literary Career." Ph.D. dissertation, Temple University, 1977 [Abstracted in Dissertation Abstracts International, 38 (October), 2117A].
   Examination of Styron's novel-in-progress, "Sophie's Choice," and of the autobiographical elements in that work and in his earlier fiction.

2 WEST, JAMES L. W., III. William Styron: A Descriptive Bibli- ography. Preface by William Styron. Boston: G.K. Hall, 252 pp.
   Extensive annotated listing of Styron's publications, including: Editions in English; Editions in French; Pre- viously Unpublished Contributions to Books and Other Publi- cations; Republished Contributions to Books; Appearances in Periodicals and Newspapers; Published Letters; Blurbs; Non-French Translations; Interviews, Published Discussions, and Published Comments; and Miscellaneous.

1977 B SHORTER WRITINGS

1 ANON. "Styron, Sweet Briar and Sophie," Sweet Briar College Alumnae Magazine, 47 (Summer), 10-13.
   Account of Styron's visit to Sweet Briar to give a reading. Includes transcription of an interview with Janet Lowrey (1977.B10, B11).

2 BERNSTEIN, JEREMY, HAROLD BLOOM, ROBERT BOYERS, et al. "Ameri- can Writers: Who's Up, Who's Down?" Esquire 88 (August), 77-81 [80].

1977

Thirty-two writers and critics talk about which writers
they like and dislike; includes George Steiner's praise of
Lie Down in Darkness as "a classic achievement."

3   BUCHWALD, ART. "Capitol Punishment--A Last Resort: The Treaty
    of Martha's Vineyard," Washington Post (7 August), p. E1.
        Syndicated humorous column in which Indians purportedly
    arrive at Styron's home on Martha's Vineyard to claim land
    they feel was illegally taken from them.

4   CERF, BENNETT. At Random--The Reminiscences of Bennett Cerf.
    New York: Random House, pp. 135, 136, 137, 238, 249, 254-
    56.
        Brief memories of going to Faulkner's funeral with Styron
    and of circumstances surrounding Styron's decision to pub-
    lish his books with Random House.

5   C[OUSINS], N[ORMAN]. "Editor's Page--When Writers Meet," Sat-
    urday Review, n.s. 4 (17 September), 8-9, 57-59 [58].
        Account of a Moscow conference of American and Soviet
    writers at which Styron was a participant. He is quoted
    briefly on the influence of television in the United States.

6   FRIEDMAN, MELVIN J. "Dislocations of Setting and Word: Notes
    on American Fiction Since 1950," Studies in American Fiction,
    5 (Spring), 79-98 [79-81, 89].
        Mention of Styron, along with John Hawkes, as two writers
    "central to the American fictional scene" who are "represen-
    tative of its possibilities and concerns" during the past
    twenty-five years. Stresses their similarities despite
    seemingly basic differences. Also brief mention of "Sophie's
    Choice."

7   GRAY, RICHARD. The Literature of Memory--Modern Writers of
    the American South. Baltimore: Johns Hopkins University
    Press, pp. 284-305.
        Reprinting of 1975.B7.

8   HALPERN, JEANNE WEINSTEIN. "Form and Image in Contemporary
    American Biography." Ph.D. dissertation, University of
    Michigan, 1977 [Abstracted in Dissertation Abstracts Inter-
    national, 38 (September), 1379A].
        Nat Turner is one of six texts studied with respect to
    "the selection and use of documentary materials, the dis-
    tribution of a life over the pages of a text, and the style
    of biographical prose."

1977

9   HOLMAN, C. HUGH. <u>The Immoderate Past--The Southern Writer and History</u>. The 1976 Lamar Lectures at Wesleyan College. Athens: University of Georgia Press, pp. 8, 10, 87-90.
     Brief consideration of <u>Nat Turner</u>. Although it is flawed by Styron's use of the single point of view "and its highly interior consciousness, which is laid before us in a language appropriate to its characters in its rhythm, but not in its complexity and figures," the novel, "for all its traditional technique, is a thoroughly modern novel."

10   LOWREY, JANET. "William Styron Reminisces," Lynchburg (Va.) <u>News</u> (24 April), pp. C-9, C-14.
     Account of Styron's visit to Sweet Briar College which includes excerpts from an interview with him.

11   _____. "A 'Transplanted Southerner' Talks About Writing," <u>Sweet Briar News</u> (29 April), p. 8.
     Account of Styron's visit to Sweet Briar College, with with excerpts from an interview with him.

12   OWNBEY, RAY. "Discussions With William Styron," <u>Mississippi Quarterly</u>, 30 (Spring), 283-95.
     Interview in which Styron speaks of "Sophie's Choice," of the reception of <u>Nat Turner</u>, of his views of the military, and of Vietnam.

13   STANFORD, MIKE. "An Interview With William Styron," <u>The Archive</u> (Duke University), 89 (Spring), 84-93.
     Styron talks about his early years at Duke, about the reception of <u>Nat Turner</u>, about "Sophie's Choice," and about the state of American fiction in 1977.

14   WATKINS, FLOYD C. "<u>The Confessions of Nat Turner</u>: History and Imagination," in his <u>In Time and Place--Some Origins of American Fiction</u>. Athens: University of Georgia Press, pp. 51-70.
     Defense of Styron's novel against the accusations of historical inaccuracy. It is "the only significant novel by a white man which attempts to recreate the immediacy and intensity...of the moment-to-moment events and thoughts of a slave" and it is valuable whether or not it is factually accurate.

15   WEST, JAMES L. W., III. "Textual Note," in <u>Christchurch--An Address Delivered at Christchurch School on May 28, 1975</u>. By William Styron. Davidson, N.C.: Briarpatch Press, p. 9.
     Brief introductory note about circumstances of the address and mention that a 104-word passage in the manuscript not read by Styron has been omitted from the text.

1978 A BOOKS – NONE

1978 B SHORTER WRITINGS

1   WEST, JAMES L. W., III. "Afterword," in <u>Admiral Robert Penn</u>
    <u>Warren and The Snows of Winter</u>. Winston-Salem, N.C.:
    Palaemon Press.
        Commentary on Styron's tribute to Warren, delivered at
    the Lotos Club in New York City on April 10, 1975.

2   WINFREY, CAREY. "Ex-Postmaster's Indictment Stirs Roxbury,"
    New York <u>Times</u> (12 January), p. 33.
        Mr. and Mrs. Styron are among the Roxbury residents who
    are quoted regarding the resignation and subsequent indict-
    ment of the town's postmaster for discarding mail.

Index

WORKS BY WILLIAM STYRON ARE LISTED IN CAPITAL LETTERS

Cheyer, A. H., 1962.B15
"Chicago 7," 1969.B19
Chisolm, Elise T., 1968.B39
Cirino, Linda D., 1976.B2
Clark, G. Glenwood, 1951.B11
Clark, Geoffrey D., 1968.B36
Clarke, Gerald, 1972.B7
Clarke, John Henrik, 1968.A1
Clarke, John Henrik (subject),
   1968.B33, B49, B59-B61,
   B87-B88, B92, B116,
   B118-B119, B125; 1969.B2, B6,
   B8, B10, B30; 1971.A2, B11,
   B36; 1975.B13; 1976.B13
Cleary, Pal, 1961.B7
Cleland, James T., 1968.B40
Clemens, Samuel (subject),
   1951.B33; 1966.B11
Clemons, Joel, 1967.B32
Coale, Samuel Chase, V, 1971.B7
Coates, John T., 1961.B8
Cockshutt, Rod, 1971.B8
Coindreau, Maurice-Edgar,
   1962.B13, B28
Cole, Verne, 1967.B33
Coleman, Elliott (subject),
   1963.B5
Coles, Robert, 1968.B41-B42
Collamore, Elizabeth, 1968.B43
Collier, Peter, 1967.B34
Collins, L. M., 1967.B35
Cominsky, J. R., 1967.B36
THE CONFESSIONS OF NAT TURNER,
   1952.B16; 1962.B11, B28-B29;
   1963.B9; 1965.B18; 1966.B3,
   B9; 1967.B1-B9, B11-B75,
   B77-B88, B90-B108, B111-B114,
   B116-B137, B139-B177;
   1968.A1-A2, B3-B8, B10-B12,
   B16, B18-B20, B22-B27,
   B30-B34, B36-B42, B44-B45,
   B47-B50, B53-B76, B79-B85,
   B87-B92, B94-B98, B100-B101,
   B103, B105-B106, B108-B111,
   B113-B120, B123-B126;
   1969.A2, B1-B3, B5-B8,
   B10-B13, B15, B17, B20, B22,
   B24-B25, B27, B30, B33-B36;
   1970.A1-A2, B2-B4, B8-B10,
   B12-B15, B20-B22, B24-B25;

1971.A1-A2, A4-A7, B4-B6, B9,
   B11-B13, B15-B16, B18,
   B22-B26, B30-B34, B36-B38;
   1972.A1-A3, B4, B11, B14,
   B16-B17; 1973.A1-A3, B7,
   B13-B15, B18, B20;
   1974.A1-A3, B3-B8, B14-B15;
   1975.A1, A3-A4, B5-B7, B11,
   B13; 1976.A2-A3, B1, B3-B4,
   B9, B12-B13; 1977.A1-A2,
   B7-B9, B12-B14
Cook, Bruce, 1967.B37
Cooke, Michael, 1968.B44;
   1969.B6
Cooper, James Fenimore (subject),
   1966.B11
Core, George, 1968.B45; 1969.B7;
   1970.B8; 1975.A4
Corodimas, Peter Nicholas,
   1972.A1
Courlander, Harold (subject),
   1967.B169
Cousins, Norman, 1977.B5
Covici, Pascal, Jr., 1960.B24
Cowley, Malcolm, 1951.B28;
   1953.B3; 1958.B3
Cowley, Malcolm (subject),
   1973.B6
Coyle, William, 1967.B38
Creed, Howard, 1960.B25
Cross, Leslie, 1951.B29
Crume, Paul, 1951.B30
Culligan, Glendy, 1960.B26
Cunliffe, Marcus, 1970.B9
Cunningham, Bill, 1960.B27
Cunningham, Dick, 1967.B39
Curley, Thomas F., 1960.B28
Currie, Edward, 1967.B40
Curtis, Bruce, 1971.B9

<u>D</u>

Dabney, Virginius, 1971.B10
Dahms, Joseph G., 1960.B29
Dana, Peake A., 1971.A1
Daniels, N. A., 1960.B30
Davidson, Ted, 1969.B8
Davis, John Roderick, 1969.B9
Davis, Paxton, 1967.B41; 1968.B46

Davis, Richard, 1951.B31
Davis, Robert Gorham, 1951.B32;
    1954.B2; 1960.B31; 1963.B8
Dawkins, Cecil, 1960.B32
Death in the Afternoon
    (Hemingway), 1973.B6
Delany, Lloyd Tom, 1968.B47
Dempsey, David, 1951.B33
Derleth, August, 1951.B34;
    1967.B42
Detweiler, Robert, 1964.B5
De Vecchi Rocca, Luisa, 1970.B10
Dickey, James (subject), 1974.B6
Didion, Joan, 1960.B33
Dillard, R. H. W., 1971.B30
DiPerna, Sharon, 1970.B11
Discovery, 1953.B1-B2, B4, B6-B7
Dixon, Donald C., 1967.B43
Doar, Harriet, 1963.B9-B10;
    1964.B6
Dommergues, Pierre, 1965.B5;
    1974.B3
Donnelly, Tom, 1951.B35
Dostoevski, Feodor (subject),
    1966.B4
Downing, Francis, 1951.B36
Downs, Lenthiel H., 1974.B7
Drake, Robert, 1968.B48
Dred (Stowe), 1970.B14
Dreiser, Theodore (subject),
    1972.B16; 1974.B15
Duberman, Martin, 1967.B44;
    1968.B49; 1969.B10; 1970.A1
Duff, John B., 1971.A2
Duffer, Ken, 1967.B45-B47
Dwight, Ogden G., 1951.B37;
    1960.B34

E

Earl, Leonard Francis, 1951.B38
Edmiston, Susan, 1976.B2
Eggenschwiler, David, 1974.B4
Ellison, Ralph (subject),
    1966.B7; 1969.B34
Elwood, Irene, 1951.B39
Emmanuel, Pierre, 1969.B11
Enright, D. J., 1968.B50
Epstein, Seymour, 1970.B12
Evans, Derro, 1960.B35

F

Fadiman, Clifton, 1967.B48
Fane, Vernon, 1952.B9
Fanning, Garth, 1967.B49
Farber, James, 1951.B40
Fauchereau, Serge, 1969.B12
Faulkner, William (subject),
    1951.B28, B31, B33, B41, B58,
    B66; 1952.B2; 1953.B5;
    1960.B102; 1962.B4-B5, B11,
    B14, B20; 1963.B15, B24;
    1965.B9, B17-B18; 1967.B139,
    B148; 1969.B32; 1970.A1;
    1971.B7, B21; 1972.B13;
    1973.B6, B16; 1974.A2, B3,
    B6; 1977.B4
Favre, Gregory, 1967.B50
Fenton, Charles A., 1960.B36
Ferguson, Anna Lawrence, 1960.B37
Ferguson, Charles A., 1967.B51
Finkelstein, Sidney, 1965.B6
Firestone, Bruce M., 1975.A1
Fitzgerald, F. Scott (subject),
    1951.B2; 1960.B55, B102;
    1969.B18; 1972.B13; 1974.A2
The Fixer (Malamud), 1971.B26;
    1974.B8
Flanders, Jane, 1976.B3
Flaubert, Gustave, (subject),
    1962.B29
Forkner, Ben, 1974.B5
Fosburgh, Lacey, 1968.B52
Fossum, Robert H., 1968.A2
Foster, Richard, 1960.B38
Fournier, Norman, 1967.B52
Fowler, Robert, 1951.B41
Franklin, Jimmy L., 1971.B11
Franklin, John Hope, 1967.B53
Fremont-Smith, Eliot,
    1967.B54-B55; 1968.B53-B54
French, Marion Flood, 1960.B39
French, Philip, 1968.B55
Friedman, Joseph J., 1957.B1
Friedman, Melvin J., 1961.B9;
    1966.B5; 1967.A1, B56;
    1968.B56; 1970.A1; 1971.B12;
    1972.B8; 1974.A2; 1977.B6
From Summer to Summer (Rose
    Styron), 1968.B21

Index

Heise, Kenan, 1967.B70
Heller, Joseph (subject),
 1964.B3; 1969.A1
Hemingway, Ernest (subject),
 1960.B68; 1973.B6; 1974.A2
Henderson, Harry B., III, 1974.B8
Herman, Dick, 1967.B71
Heth, Edward Harris, 1951.B53
Hicks, Granville, 1960.B46;
 1967.B72-B73
Hicks, Walter J., 1967.B74
Hiers, John Turner, 1974.B9;
 1975.B8
Higby, Jim, 1967.B75
Highet, Gilbert, 1960.B47
Hill, Bob, 1951.B54
Hill, Susan, 1961.B14
Hilzim, William H., 1968.A3
Hodgart, Patricia, 1968.B74
Hodges, Betty, 1959.B4;
 1960.B48-B49; 1968.B75-B76
Hoerchner, Susan Jane, 1974.B10
Hoey, Reid A., 1960.B50
Hoffman, Frederick J., 1961.B24;
 1963.B13; 1967.A1, B76;
 1968.B77; 1970.A1
Hogan, William, 1967.B77-B78
Holder, Alan, 1969.B15
Hollander, John, 1960.B51
Holley, Fred S., 1953.B6
Holman, C. Hugh, 1969.B7; 1977.B9
Homsy, Jerry, 1965.B9
Hooker, Pat, 1959.B5
Horan, Kenneth, 1951.B55
Howard, Jane, 1968.B78
Hoyt, Charles Alva, 1967.B79
Hoyt, Elizabeth North, 1951.B56;
 1967.B80
Hubbell, Jay B., 1972.B10
Hughes, David, 1962.B19
Hummel, Joseph W., 1960.B52
Humphrey, William (subject),
 1975.B8
Hunt, Howard, 1951.B57
Hunter, Anna C., 1960.B53
Hurt, Richard L., 1967.B81
Hutchens, John K., 1951.B58;
 1960.B54
Hutchinson, Ruth, 1960.B55
Hux, Samuel H., 1966.B7

I

Inge, M. Thomas, 1971.B17
Ingle, H. L., 1967.B82
IN THE CLAP SHACK, 1971.B2;
 1972.B3, B5, B9; 1973.B1-B2,
 B5, B8, B12, B19; 1974.B11;
 1975.A4; 1976.A2
Invisible Man (Ellison), 1953.B3;
 1969.B34
Irving, Clifford (subject),
 1972.B9
István, Hermann, 1966.B8

J

Jacobs, Robert D., 1961.B24
James, Henry (subject), 1960.B68
Janeway, Elizabeth, 1952.B12
Johansson, Eric, 1963.B14
Johnson, C. W., 1960.B56
Johnson, Pamela Hansford,
 1952.B13
Johnson, Stanley, 1951.B59
Jones, Carter Brooke, 1951.B60;
 1960.B57
Jones, Howard Mumford, 1951.B61
Jones, James (subject), 1963.B28
Jones, Madison, 1960.B105
Joyce, James (subject), 1951.B33;
 1970.A1
Juin, Herbert, 1962.B20

K

Kaiser, Ernest, 1968.A1; 1970.A1
Kaufman, Clarence, 1960.B58
Kauffmann, Stanley, 1967.B83
Kaufmann, Walter, 1968.B79
Kazin, Alfred, 1959.B6; 1962.B21;
 1967.B84; 1971.B18
Kelley, James E., 1951.B62
Kelly, Frederic, 1966.B9
Kelvin, Norman, 1975.A4
Kennedy, Edward (subject),
 1973.B3
Kenney, Herbert, Jr., 1960.B59
Keown, Don, 1967.B85

148

Monaghan, Charles, 1960.B83;
  1968.B93
Moody, Minnie Hite, 1967.B108
Mooney, Harry, Jr., 1960.B84
Moore, John Rees, 1961.B17;
  1971.B30
Moore, L. Hugh, 1965.B13
Moreland, John, 1960.B85
Morgan, Henry Grady, Jr.,
  1973.A1
Morgan-Powell, S., 1951.B75
Morris, Robert K., 1975.A4
Morris, Willie, 1967.B109-B110
Morris, Willie (subject),
  1966.B10; 1971.B8
Morrissy, W. B., 1951.B76
Morse, J. Mitchell, 1969.B20
Morton, James Parks, 1974.B12
Morton, Joseph J., 1951.B77
Mossman, Josef, 1951.B78
Moyano, Maria Clara, 1967.B111
Moynahan, Julian, 1968.B94
Moynihan, John, 1968.B95
Mozart, Wolfgang Amadeus
  (subject), 1965.B16
Mudrick, Marvin, 1964.B12;
  1970.B15
Mulchrone, Vincent, 1968.B96
Mullen, Jean S., 1971.B24
Munn, L. S., 1951.B79
Murray, Albert, 1967.B112;
  1971.A2
Murray, James G., 1960.B86
Murrell, Helen, 1967.B113
Myers, Arthur, 1967.B114

N

Nelson, Doris L., 1970.B16
Nelson, Norman K., 1951.B80
Nenadal, Rodoslav, 1975.B9
Newberry, Mike, 1960.B87
Newcomb, Horace, 1968.B97
Newman, Marc, 1970.A1
Nichols, Lewis, 1960.B88;
  1962.B30
Nichols, Luther, 1960.B89
Nicholson, Henry, 1951.B81
Nigro, August, 1966.A1; 1967.A1,
  B115

Noggle, Burt, 1963.B20
Nolte, William H., 1967.B116;
  1973.B14
Norman, Sue, 1960.B90
Normand, Jean, 1969.B21; 1974.B13
North, Sterling, 1951.B82

O

Oates, Stephen B., 1973.B15
O'Brien, Alfred, Jr., 1951.B83
O'Brien, E. D., 1961.B20
O'Connell, Shaun V., 1965.B14;
  1967.B117; 1970.A2; 1975.B10
O'Connor, Flannery, 1960.B105
O'Connor, Flannery (subject),
  1959.B6; 1971.B7; 1975.B8
O'Connor, Richard, 1951.B84
O'Connor, William Van, 1964.B13
O'Dell, Scott, 1951.B85
Okogbue C., 1976.B9
Olderman, Raymond M., 1972.B15
O'Leary, Theodore M., 1951.B86;
  1960.B91
Oliver, Jane Sidney, 1969.A3
Oliver, Joan, 1951.B87
Ol' Prophet Nat (Panger),
  1967.B47; 1968.B75
One and Twenty: Duke Narrative
  and Verse, 1924-1946,
  1946.B1
Oppenheimer, Martin, 1965.B15
O'Rourke, Elizabeth, 1959.B8
Osborne, Lorraine, 1967.B118
Ottaway, Robert, 1968.B98
Ownbey, Ray Wilson, 1972.A2;
  1977.B12

P

Pace, Norma W., 1951.B89
Panger, Daniel (subject),
  1967.B47; 1968.B75
Paris Review, 1953.B1, B8;
  1958.B2; 1963.B9, B28
Parke, Mary Eugenia, 1951.B90;
  1953.B7-B8; 1954.B4
Parker, Roy, Jr., 1967.B119
Parks, Carole A., 1968.B36

151